COINAGE

IN THE

GREEK

WORLD

COINAGE
— IN THE —
GREEK WORLD

Ian Carradice &
Martin Price

Seaby
LONDON

Typeset by Photosetting & Secretarial Services, 6 Foundry House,
Stars Lane, Yeovil, Somerset BA20 1NL
and printed and bound in Great Britain
by Billings & Sons Ltd, Worcester
for the publishers
B. A. Seaby Ltd.
8 Cavendish Square
London W1M 0AJ

Distributed by
B. T. Batsford Ltd.
P. O. Box 4, Braintree, Essex CM7 7QY

Carradice, Ian
Coinage in the Greek world.
1. Ancient Greek coins
I. Title   II. Price, M. Jessop (Martin Jessop), 1939–
737.4938

ISBN 0 900652 82 9 ✓

Contents

Preface

The world of the Greeks spread from Spain to India and from Russia to Egypt. Within this wide geographical span coinage was issued by empires and minor monarchies and by large and small city states, leaving for us today a bewildering array of little objects in a variety of metals and sizes. This slim book has arranged the material so that the collector and the student will have an overview of the development of this monetary medium placed within the cultural spheres in which coins originated.

There is a fascination exerted by these objects out of all proportion to their size, and the reader is here introduced to some of the facets of the interest engendered by coins. Every coin that has survived is part of history. Each coin was made for a purpose and the devices placed upon it were consciously chosen to express the authority of the issuer. Through these myriad designs we can look back into the Greek world to search for the stories behind the coins and for the people who made and used them.

CHAPTER 1

Progress in the study of Greek coinage

Hardly a day passes in the 1980s without there being some discovery in the field of Greek coinage. New evidence in the form of newly-discovered coin designs or of new coin hoards and other finds leads to a continuous reevaluation of the relationship of coins to the historical and artistic context of the place in which they were made. This in turn enables the numismatist to construct a picture that is always changing as the web of intricate evidence is pieced together. For the historian or collector the present revolution created by the necessary reassessment of the evidence in all periods of Greek coinage may cause embarrassment or confusion; but for the student closely involved with new ideas and new evidence there is the excitement of being present as our knowledge and understanding of this aspect of the Greek world are extended. However, it is important that numismatics does not become a subject separate from history and archaeology. The tendency towards specialization must be constantly bridged by an awareness that this is only one of many facets of the ancient world, and that the study of Greek coinage can help to throw light on a variety of aspects of the Greek civilization.

The beginnings of Greek numismatics

The attraction of coins as relics of past history to a great extent lies in the direct contact that they convey with the peoples of the past. The Roman emperor Augustus was fascinated by the portraits of earlier rulers, and he sought to share his enthusiasm by giving out old coins to his guests as presents at the Saturnalia festival – Christmas-tide. In the Renaissance it was again the iconography, and particularly the portraits of Roman emperors, which fired the interest of those who sought to increase their knowledge of the ancient world. Imagination and wishful thinking have

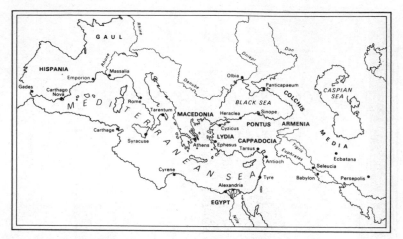

Fig. 1 *The Greek World*

always played a part in the study of the past. Today we may laugh at our early predecessors who saw in the radiate bust of Helios on coins of Rhodes (**263**) the face of Christ wearing the crown of thorns, and who concluded that the coins were therefore the money paid to the traitor Judas. This is, however, a salient reminder that each generation must rethink the accepted traditions of earlier generations, aware of the limitations imposed by modern preconceptions and inadequate evidence. The prime task of the numismatist, in the Renaissance as now, is to identify and date the coins and to have a clear picture of the details of the designs. Only then can the coins be used for a broader understanding of their civilization. In the seventeenth century great collections began to be formed. Improvements in travel and communications, and the opening up of the eastern Mediterranean to the Grand Tour, created a steady stream of new material coming to northern Europe. Catalogues by Hubert Goltz (1526-83), Jean Vaillant (1632-1706), Joseph Pellerin (1684-1782), Joseph Eckhel (1737-98) (*see* **Fig. 2**), and Domenico Sestini (1750-1823) bear witness to the new passion for collecting coins, and these form the basis from which our present understanding has grown.

The national collections of today, which provide the stimulus and facilities for research, are the heritage of the great royal collections of Europe. In France, Pellerin, himself an avid collector who formed a cabinet of more than thirty two thousand coins, became the Keeper of the Royal Collection. By linking this to his own, the foundations of the great collection in the Bibliothèque Nationale, Paris were laid. In Britain,

Fig. 2   *Engraving of Joseph Eckhel (1737-98), at work on the Imperial Collection in Vienna*

the collections of keen antiquarians were donated or purchased for the nation, and in 1814 the first catalogue of the British Museum collection of Greek coins was produced. More than half the coins came from the bequest of Dean Cracherode in 1799. This in turn stimulated interest in these objects and by 1850 a vast number of coins had been acquired, including the collections of well known diplomats such as Robert Ainslie and Lord Elgin, and the Royal Collection. In Vienna, Eckhel put in order the large Imperial Collection of the Holy Roman Empire. With the organization stemming from the catalogues of these collections, the scientific study of Greek numismatics was born.

To some extent numismatics still suffers from one of the problems evident in the eighteenth century. Sestini, who travelled widely in Greek lands, was able to appreciate from the find spots of coins the probable location of their mint. In the twentieth century, Louis Robert has underlined again and again the importance of field research. The curators of the great coin cabinets still suffer from the limitations of the armchair, studying their coins and their archives without the close contact with the places where the coins are found. Those who do live and travel in these lands have an important role to play in our understanding of the objects.

The size and complexity of national coin collections has, in many cases, resulted in their separation from other artefacts of the ancient world, and an unfortunate consequence of this has been that numismatics has become a separate study. It is of paramount importance that this necessary specialization be carefully controlled and it is the duty of the numismatist constantly to expound for the historian and archaeologist the developments in the subject.

Together with the creation of national coin collections, the nineteenth century saw the growth of numismatic societies in several countries in order to foster research in the subject, and the annual journal became the medium through which the results of research could be regularly published. With the production of sulphur casts, and later electrotype copies and plaster casts, material could be concentrated in one place from many different sources, and a list such as that of Theodore Mionnet (1770-1842) of some fifty two thousand Greek coins underlines how important it is to gather as much material as possible before seeking to launch into its interpretation.

Die links

The introduction of the published photograph pioneered by B.V. Head (1844-1914) in his study of Syracuse, in the Numismatic Chronicle of 1874, provided a momentous breakthrough for the study of coins. The line drawings that had previously been used to illustrate scholars' discussions could give only a basic view of the iconography. The photograph placed in the hands of the scholar everything, except perhaps the fabric, which is required for the full study of the object.

This innovation coincided with the recognition that it was possible to identify coins struck from the very same die. In the Numismatic Chronicle of 1869, E.H. Bunbury published such a link between two coins of Lysimachus which had recently been attributed to separate mints. The Swiss collector and scholar, F. Imhoof Blumer, began to use this new tool to establish the chronology and mint city of different issues of Alexander the Great (232-3). Style had long been used as a major criterion for establishing a chronological relationship for coins. The work of individual artists may be identified from a close inspection of their products, but to some extent this approach suffers from the subjective view of the student. The die link between two objects provides a more empirical and trustworthy piece of evidence. On the assumption that the die itself had a limited period of use and would not normally travel from place to place, the link could be used to bring clarity to the relative sequence of coin issues.

The first monographs to use the new tool of die linking as the prime element in the organization of the material were those of K. Regling on Terina (1906) and P. Lederer on Segesta (1910). From these small beginnings major studies, such as E. Boehringer's Syracuse (1929) and G. Le Rider's Philip II (1977), show the prime importance of organizing large quantities of material by careful and detailed analysis of dies. It is in this way essential that the numismatist be able to grasp the minutiae of individual die strikings – the pattern of which may be extremely complicated – and at the same time to maintain the overall view of the groups of issues in the broader contexts of history and archaeology.

Hoards

Along with the study of dies, the twentieth century has recognized the importance for chronology and other problems of studying hoards and contexts in excavations in which coins are found.

The first hoard to be described in detail in post-classical times is also a record of the largest hoard ever found. On 12 June 1366, at Tourves, fifty kilometres east of Marseilles, children came across some coins which had fallen from a small hole. When they enlarged the hole with their hands coins proceeded to shower from the side of the bank 'like a water fountain'. The shower continued for some time, and when the silver was collected it required twenty mules to carry it off. It has been estimated that the weight must have been in the region of two thousand four hundred kilogrammes. The coin type was described and can be identified as an obol of Massalia which weighed only half a gramme. The deposit must have contained some four million pieces! There were few hoards published in detail in the eighteenth century, but that from Latakia, published by Pellerin in 1765 with good line drawings of the coins, is a model publication. It is interesting to compare the illustrations with those of Henri Seyrig's republication of the hoard in 1973 using photographs taken from plaster casts. Scholars became increasingly aware that hoards, and particularly those taken direct from circulation, provided useful information on the relative sequence of the issues. On the assumption that the most recently struck coins may be the least worn, the study of the pieces found in hoard contexts can be added to the evidence gleaned from the study of style and die links to create an accurate impression of the history of the coinage. It is also a common phenomenon that coins representing the most recently minted examples in a hoard often stem from a limited number of dies, which gives further detailed information on the sequence of issues.

It is often possible to show that a hoard had been accumulated as savings over a generation or more. Older coins put away for safekeeping in earlier years would see none of the wear of coins in continuous circulation and so may appear as little worn as the latest coins in a hoard. A poignant description of such a hoard occurs in a papyrus from Egypt dated AD 28/9, in which Orsenouphis complains of the theft during building work of a hoard secreted by his mother in 15 BC. It consisted of gold earrings, a gold crescent ornament, a pair of silver arm bracelets weighing twelve drachmae, a necklace worth eighty drachmae and sixty drachmae in silver coins. His knowledge of where the hoard lay underlines that he could have added coins to it over forty years after its original burial. A single coin or a group of coins may be added to a family's savings long after the deposit of the first pieces. An element of common sense must always be used in evaluating the evidence of a hoard for chronological purposes. Where royal coinages are concerned, when the coins can be dated within the reigns of particular monarchs, the element of accumulation may be obvious and causes no problem. In the majority of cases, however, it is important to reserve judgement on the evidence of a single hoard before jumping to apparently obvious conclusions and to balance all the evidence, and particularly the evidence of all recorded hoards.

By their very nature hoards are unpredictable, although after two hundred years of study the circulation patterns in different areas of the Greek world are fairly well known. A hoard from Larissa in Thessaly in 1968 produced more than fifteen hundred examples of a drachma of Rhodian types (**265**) signed by Hermias as the person responsible for the issue, and with the letters ZΩ replacing the PO of Rhodes. No example of this variety had been published, but research elicited that two examples had previously survived. With such a rare issue it was therefore not surprising to find that all the examples in the hoard were from only three obverse and two reverse dies. This chance discovery changed the coins from being exceedingly rare to being fairly common, although it was clear that the issue was one of short duration. The fact that so many pieces were found in Thessaly confirmed the evidence of a most unusual style to show that the issue was not in fact made on the island of Rhodes. Indeed, the ethnic had been replaced by the letters ZΩ and the issue clearly belonged with a group of similar pieces of the same Rhodian types, but which have been identified as local imitations of Rhodian coins. One of the two previously known examples also came from a hoard, found at Metsovon in Macedonia, and this confirms both the general area of manufacture as well as the date of issue. There can be no doubt that the Hermias variety was made in central or North Greece during or immediately before the final war between Rome and Macedonia (172-168 BC). The Metsovon hoard was buried during the war and the Larissa hoard, containing the latest coins of King Perseus and issues of the First Macedonian Republic, was buried just after it. The remarkable group of the issue of Hermias had been held by the owner of the Larissa hoard for a few years before its final burial.

Scholarship consists of asking the right questions and, once the problems of date and place of mintage have been satisfactorily solved, further questions arise concerning the iconography, metrology or, when names occur, the prosopography. In the case of Hermias, a prime historical question is: why were such pieces made in Greece in imitation of Rhodian coins? This can be linked to a further question that can be asked of every coin issue: what was its function? There are few references to the issue of coins in ancient sources and the patterns built up from hoards can be very useful. The time and place of issue clearly play a role, as do the denominations chosen. A ten-drachma represents a payment very different from an obol (a sixth of a drachma).

The 'Rhodian' group, of which the Hermias forms a part, is a sufficiently unusual phenomenon to warrant inclusion in the discussion. Clearly the payment in this type of coin was demanded or preferred by those who were to benefit from it. Official Rhodian coins played no part in the general coin circulation of mainland Greece. The name of Hermias linked with the letters Zo ... is also a clue to the origin of the issue. It happens that at this very time a certain Hermias, son of Zoilos from the city of Oropos in Boeotia, is known from an inscription at Delphi to have been a partisan of Perseus, King of Macedonia. There is every probability that this extraordinary group of issues was created in the context of the war with Rome. The denomination struck is consistent with payments to troops on a regular basis, and the hypothesis that Hermias may have been responsible for paying a band of mercenaries, possibly from Rhodes, is an attractive starting point on which further research may build.

Overstrikes

In addition to hoards, and to the analysis of dies and style, the numismatist has other tools with which to construct a chronology. At certain times those responsible for the production of coinage used other coins as flans on which to strike new designs. These might be old issues of the same state or coins from elsewhere of the correct weight or module. One thing is certain: the designs of the 'overstrike' must be later in time than those of the 'undertype' (**57**). With issues from the same city, the relative sequence is assured. When the undertype is from elsewhere the relative sequence is also assured, but in addition the chronological sequence of the city using the new designs is locked into the sequence of the place of the original issue. All the evidence that can be brought to bear on the one can to some extent be used to throw light on the other.

The chronology of the New Style coinage of Athens was carefully analysed in a model mint study by Margaret Thompson in 1962. Prior to this publication, the exceptional issue of Athenian gold and silver coins bearing the name of King Mithradates (**244**) was believed to belong to the time when Mithradates VI of Pontus occupied Athens (88–86 BC). The hoards appeared to confirm this and scholars accepted this as a firm fixed point in the chronology. The importance of an overstruck coin in the Berlin collection was only recognized by Miss Thompson. An Athenian tetradrachm, which must be placed on the evidence of style and hoards some time after that of Mithradates, was found to have been overstruck by a Macedonian tetradrachm in the name of the Roman quaestor Aesillas (**239**). This man is not known from other historical sources, but his coinage had consistently been dated to the time of Mithradates' invasion of Greece in 88 BC or a little before. Miss Thompson could see no reason to change the date of Aesillas' period of office. The effect of the existence of this one overstruck coin was dramatic. The issues in the name of Mithradates could no longer be linked to Mithradates VI but had to be linked to his predecessor, Mithradates V. All the other evidence was reevaluated and a radically new chronology was constructed. The relative sequence of the various issues of the New Style coinage remained unchanged. The absolute chronology was placed several years earlier in order to accommodate the Aesillas issue of about 88 BC. The scholastic world reacted in disbelief at this revolution and even today the matter has not been fully resolved. However, it is now widely accepted that the evidence for the chronology of the Athenian New Style issues from other sources is too strong to allow the date of the Aesillas issue to remain at its traditional point of 88 BC. Recent finds combining the coins of Aesillas with closely datable Roman denarii allow a redating of the crucial Aesillas issue to the mid 70s BC, at the time when Mithradates was yet again threatening the stability of the Roman provinces.

Hoards containing coins from many different states, overstrikes by coins of one city upon those of another, designs borrowed by one city from another, or designs adopted by agreement or treaty, all create a finely interwoven network of evidence upon which the structure of Greek coinage is built.

'Fixed' points in the chronology

The political history derived from written sources – historical texts and inscriptions – can be linked into the numismatic chronology at a number of points so that the absolute dating of the issues can be gauged and their historical significance evaluated. In the nineteenth century, before the tools of the numismatist had woven the structure that we have today, it was these key chronological points which attracted scholars – particularly those few occasions when the striking of coins is mentioned in historical sources (*see* chapter 2). Aristotle's assumption that Solon's reform of weights and measures included a coinage became a terminus ante quem for Athenian coinage itself. Pheidon's translation of spits into coinage set the historical context for the introduction of coinage at Argos. The donation by Croesus of gold staters to the people of Delphi made the attribution to him of the earliest gold coins, the lion and bull forepart issues of Sardes, extremely plausible. The golden crown which Queen Demarete of Syracuse turned into donative ten-drachma pieces (*see* chapter 3) became inextricably linked with the earliest of Syracuse's fine silver decadrachms.

In each case the coins were fitted to the historical setting, and since these identifications have held the stage for more than a century, it is only with the greatest difficulty that numismatists of today can persuade historians that the assumptions of past generations have no basis in fact. That a gold crown cannot be melted down into silver decadrachms is no obstacle to the enthusiasm of a nineteenth century romantic determined to bring the past to life. It is essential, however, if the truth is to be recovered, to consider impartially the date of the issue of the coins using the tools that are at hand before assuming that they fit this or that historical context.

All assumptions must be kept in train. Hoards may or may not have been deposited in a time of war or crisis. The fact that the owner did not return to retrieve his coins does not mean that he died a sudden or violent death – merely that he did not tell anyone where the hoard lay. It is remarkable that the Peloponnesian War, which disrupted the Greek world at the end of the fifth century BC, appears to have had little effect on the pattern of hoarding. While many cities had to strike coinage in order to be able to have troops in the field during a time of war, the Spartans succeeded in defeating the Athenians in the Peloponnesian War without striking a single coin.

Even the subjection or destruction of one city by another did not necessarily mean that autonomous coinage suddenly ceased. The conqueror may indeed take over for his own use the source of silver that had been used by the other, but he may also prefer to leave the existing economy to fend for itself. The Persians issued no royal coins in the eastern satrapies of their empire, and imitations of Athenian coins (**160-164**) rather than a royal Achaemenid coinage were used as currency in areas such as Mesopotamia. It was, however, expedient to have a royal coinage in the satrapy of Sardes from the sixth century BC. There can have been no suggestion that it was insulting to the Great King that Greek cities within the Persian empire should strike flourishing coinages while he had none in Persia. Modern assumptions on the need for coinage or on its propaganda value have no place in modern numismatic thinking. Coins are to be placed in their ancient context, and such light as they throw on the history of their times is to be gleaned with as little preconception as possible.

The designs used for coinage provide a rich mine of research for archaeologists. The historical and economic needs of the state determined the existence of coins of a particular denomination, and the choice of design was consciously made. The great variety of designs provides a remarkable, closely dated array of heads, objects and mythological scenes over a period of a thousand years, such as no other artefact can match. The study of buildings on coins has revealed some eight hundred different representations, many of them very schematic when reduced to the size of a coin flan, but nonetheless useful indications of details allowing reconstruction of structures long since destroyed. Ships of different types, periods and areas provide similarly useful information. Weapons of various sorts, musical instruments, vases and copies of statues all exist in sufficient detail to offer a great deal of information to the archaeologist. The coins, once studied by the numismatist, can often be dated with a fair accuracy and their place of origin can be pinpointed with certainty in the majority of cases. A great deal remains to be done before the interest of coins is exhausted.

Trends for the future

The later twentieth century has brought two further tools to help in research. The analysis of the metals is being perfected and is beginning to be of use in our understanding of the sources from which the metals came. Where there is debasement the analysis can be used to help with the dating of the coins themselves. The use of scientific analysis in the detection of forgeries is also progressing. Modern forgeries have plagued the study since the seventeenth century, but today defences are being constructed. Knowledge of what is possible and not possible in the manufacture of a particular piece is growing. Even the file marks surviving on the face of the original die, smoothed before any engraving took place, can now be photographed in magnification on the coins which it struck and used to compare with those on a new or suspect piece purporting to be from the same die.

The computer is beginning to help with the handling of large quantities of material and with the analysis of different aspects. Useful compilations already exist to help with the study of iconography and, as improvements take place in the storage of photographic images, the computer would seem to have tremendous potential in helping with the study of dies and style. All that lies in the future and, as more and more material is retrieved and recorded, the study of coinage will continue to flourish to the benefit of many aspects of our knowledge of the ancient world.

CHAPTER 2

The introduction of coinage

The first coins were made in western Asia Minor (modern Turkey) shortly before 600BC. At that time the eastern Aegean coast and islands were inhabited by Greeks who had been colonising the region for centuries; while inland the major power was the kingdom of Lydia, with its capital at Sardes. In the course of the next three centuries the use of coined money was to spread in all directions: north to parts of what is now southern Russia, to Egypt in the south, eastwards as far as Persia and westwards along the coasts of the Mediterranean Sea as far as Spain. The many and varied coinages that resulted are all classified under the general heading 'Greek', because it was under the influence of Greek culture that the designs and techniques of minting spread across the Mediterranean and beyond.

Money before coinage

Money existed long before coinage was invented. From prehistoric to modern times a wide range of objects or commodities other than coins have at some time been used by various communities as money: for example, cowrie shells and bronze tools in the ancient Far East, gold rings in ancient Egypt, dried fish in medieval Iceland and, more recently, strings of shell beads (wampum) or blankets among tribes of North American Indians and salt in nineteenth century Ethiopia. In Homeric Greece cattle were recognized as a standard measure of value; also weapons, slaves and clothing could be used and tripods and other bronze vessels were given as prizes or in payments of, for instance, compensation or ransom. The *Iliad*, Book 23, describes the prize at a wrestling match as a 'large cauldron with three legs to stand over a fire, worth twelve oxen as valued by the Achaeans', and a skilled slave girl,

Fig. 3 *The invention of coinage in western Asia Minor*

promised as a prize by Achilles, was valued at four oxen.

In addition to these 'primitive' forms of currency, the ancient civilisations of the Middle East also used weighed amounts of metal, the forerunners of true coins. The earliest cuneiform documents from Mesopotamia, dating from the middle of the third millennium BC, include accounts which record the use of weighed silver, and from Egypt the earliest evidence for weighed metal in payments is almost as ancient.

The Old Testament provides numerous references to the practice of using weighed metals. The earliest is the purchase by Abraham (in about 1900 BC) of a burial plot for his wife Sarah with a payment of four hundred shekels of silver 'current with the merchant' (*Genesis* 23, 15-16).

Examples of the ancient artefacts used in pre-coinage monetary transactions also survive. From Mesopotamia there are weights in stone and bronze, carved in the shapes of animals such as geese and lions, which were officially used to fix values. The talent of about thirty kilogrammes was the largest unit of weight in the ancient Mesopotamian system. Like the hours of the day it was divided according to the sexagesimal system, with its sixtieth part being the mina and with the mina made up of sixty shekels. From excavations at Ugarit in northern Syria weights in stone and bronze of various shapes and sizes have been unearthed, dating from about 1300 BC, together with the bronze pans of weighing scales and the grains of silver that were once weighed on them. In Ugarit the talent contained three thousand shekels, there being fifty shekels to the mina instead of the sixty in Mesopotamia. Other variations on the Mesopotamian weight system developed and it is these and other traditional weight systems which later formed the bases for many of the coinage weight standards of the ancient Greek world. Most of the terms which later came to be used to identify the various denominations of coinage (*see* chapter 6) originally derived from the practice of weighing: in the East, *shekel* = 'to weigh'; in Greek lands, *stater* = 'that which balances the scales', *drachma* = 'handful' (of objects for weighing). A more recent example is the English *pound*.

Precious metals came to be accepted as the standard medium for monetary transactions because their recognized intrinsic worth enabled them to represent relatively large values in a small, durable and portable form. The essential difference between a nugget of metal used as money and a true coin was that the coin was pre-weighed to a recognized standard usually in a system of denominations and was stamped with a mark of identification that, within the area of influence of the stamp, theoretically enabled it to change hands without the need of further weighing. However, the development from the practice of weighing anonymous metal nuggets to the acceptance of pre-stamped pieces was a slow process. Pre-coin nuggets of precious metal and true coins bearing recognizable marks of identification have been found together in hoards, and the coins stamped by different authorities would still have had to be weighed in order to establish their value before they could change hands outside their native localities. The invention of coinage did not by any means spell the end of the age-old practice of weighing in transactions. In many areas coinage continued to be regarded as bullion for years to come.

The literary traditions

One of the earliest explicit statements on the invention of coinage comes from the famous Greek historian Herodotus, the 'Father of History'. He says that 'the Lydians were the first people we know to have struck and used coinage of silver and gold' (*Herodotus* 1, 94). Herodotus was a native of Halicarnassus in Caria (south-western Turkey), a city which just two generations before his time had been part of the kingdom of Lydia. Another Greek from western Asia Minor, the mid-sixth century philosopher Xenophanes of Colophon, is also quoted as confirming the tradition which associated the Lydians with the invention of coinage. But this was not the only ancient tradition for the invention of coinage in the Greek world. Julius Pollux, writing in the second century AD (*Onomasticon* 9, 83), provides a list of the various other claimants to this invention, which includes King Pheidon of Argos (perhaps in *c.*700 BC in Aegina), the Athenians, the Naxians and King Demodike of Cyme. By the time Pollux was writing, coinage was already a very ancient invention, the origins of which were obviously no longer clearly remembered. Nowadays, only the Lydian tradition and the tradition of King Pheidon's coinage, which can be traced back as far as the fifth century BC, are given much credibility. It is thought that even Greeks of the fourth century BC could be mistaken about the early history of coinage. In the *Constitution of Athens*, attributed to Aristotle, it is stated that among other things the great Athenian lawgiver Solon reformed the coinage, probably in 594 BC, thus implying that Athenian coinage must already have been in existence by then. Yet few modern scholars now believe this could have been possible, because the evidence provided by the surviving coinage, at least as interpreted by numismatists and archaeologists, does not seem to allow such an early date for Athenian coinage. Some scholars still attempt to uphold the traditions recorded in ancient literary sources, but others, who would rather date the earliest coins by working back with numismatic evidence from later, more securely dated periods of coinage, prefer either to reinterpret the literary sources or, in some cases, deny their credibility altogether. One familiar reinterpretation of the alleged coinage activities of Pheidon and Solon is to argue that these really concerned pre-coinage weight standards and not coinage itself.

Returning to the comments of Herodotus, it is worth noting that he referred to 'coinage of silver and gold', because the earliest coins of all were not made of either of these precious metals in their pure states but of electrum. Electrum is an alloy of gold and silver, otherwise known as white gold, which occurs naturally in the sands of several rivers in Asia Minor including the Pactolus, which flowed through Sardes, the Lydian capital. By the time of Herodotus the early electrum coinage had been replaced nearly everywhere by silver and (to a much lesser extent) gold, so it is usually thought that Herodotus is not making a distinction between gold and silver, as opposed to electrum coinage, but is referring simply to the invention of coinage in general.

The earliest finds

The most important find so far of early electrum coins was made during the British Museum's excavations at Ephesus, on the Ionian coast of Asia Minor, in 1904-5. In the excavations on the site of the Temple of Artemis, at least ninety three electrum pieces, mainly small fractions, were found, mostly stamped with primitive designs but some without, as well as seven unstamped silver nuggets. In the oldest structure on the site, the Central Basis, twenty four of the electrum and four silver pieces were discovered, together with jewellery and other artefacts, in circumstances that suggest they were part of a votive foundation deposit, an offering to the goddess Artemis. A date of about 600BC has been argued for the burial of this particular deposit. The other coins from the site, including a pot hoard of nineteen pieces, are all broadly related to the Basis material and some, in fact, were struck from the same dies as coins from the Basis.

Altogether, the 'pre-coin' and coin finds from the Artemision can be divided into the following groups:

1 Seven unmarked lumps of silver of apparently regular weights.
2 Two unmarked electrum pieces with weights approximating to fractions of the 'Milesian' (or 'Lydian') stater (14.1 grammes).
3 Three electrum pieces with a simple punch mark on one side, weighing out as 'Milesian' fractions (1).
4 Four electrum pieces with a simple punch or punches on one side and a 'design' of roughly parallel striations impressed on the other side (again fractions of 'Milesian' weight) (2-3).
5 About twenty electrum pieces with punches on one side and a design on the other side consisting of an animal or animal forepart formed within a striated background (again all 'Milesian' fractions) (4).
6 More than sixty electrum pieces with punches on one side and a recognizable design on the other side, usually consisting of an animal or animal part on a plain background. Two pieces had weights equivalent to fractions of the 'Phocaic' stater (16.1 grammes); the remainder were again 'Milesian' fractions.

It is significant that unstruck nuggets and struck coins were found together in the deposits in the foundations of the Artemision, and since none of the pieces displayed any signs of wear through circulation they could not have been deposited long after the introduction of the technique that allows us to use the word 'coin'. The Artemision finds clearly illustrate this technical development. The simplest form of coin was a pre-weighed piece with a simple punch. It has been suggested that the punch originally developed because of the need to combat fraud, in the form of plating with a precious metal over a base metal core. The punch mark exposes the interior of the nugget, and so even the simplest punch could act as a mark of guarantee in the same way as the later true coin design. The principle is the same as for seals, which had been in regular use for centuries before the development of coinage. Some of the Artemision pieces from group 4 display both the mark of a punch and, on the other side, a 'design' of simple striations. These striations resulted from the electrum nugget being punched while placed on a surface scored with rough lines, probably to prevent the nugget from slipping while the punch was hammered in from above. Thus a 'coin' was produced with marks on both sides. This process of manufacture is called striking, and the two surfaces which mark the coin are called dies; the upper is the punch die and the lower is often called the anvil die. This technique of using dies to stamp the ingot or 'flan' is still used today, having survived the introduction of modern-style machinery for coining in the sixteenth and seventeenth centuries.

The designs on coins are given the name 'types' from the Greek word τύπος , meaning the effect or imprint of a blow. Recognizable types can be seen on Artemision coins from groups 5 and 6 above. In the earliest phases of coinage the type is usually found only on one side of the coin. This side, which received its type from the impression cut into the anvil die, is known as the obverse. The other side of the coin, which received the blow of the punch or punch die, is known as the reverse. Most early punches were not carved with representational designs and so the mark of the roughly engraved punch does not usually have what we would call a type. The end of the reverse punch was, however, usually rough or engraved with a pattern of uneven depressions to prevent slippage in striking, and some rare examples do contain within them tiny figures, which are the forerunners of the later reverse design.

Almost all the coins from the Artemision are not inscribed and few can be attributed with any measure of certainty to a particular issuing authority. The most simple pieces (from groups 1-4) offer no clues to their origins other than the location in which they were found. From groups 5 and 6, containing the coins with representational designs, a total of thirteen major types have been identified, but few of these can be related to later city coinages of the area. The commonest pieces were those with a lion's head in profile (nineteen examples) or with a lion's paw (twenty two examples). Comparisons of size and weight suggest that these were probably different denominations from the same series. The lion's head type (**5-6**) is by far the commonest and most widespread of all the early electrum coins from Asia Minor, and it has therefore been attributed to the kingdom of Lydia, the major power in the area. If the Basis deposits from the Artemision are to be dated to the early sixth century BC, these coins should then represent the issues of the Lydians from the time of King Alyattes (*c.*610-560 BC). Another coin type from the Artemision apparently linked to the common lion's head series has two lion heads, though only one is often visible, and an inscription down the centre which can be read as WALWEL (**7**). This was once thought to refer to King Alyattes, but the appearance of another name, KALIL, on a similar issue seems to confirm that these cannot be royal names. They might instead have been the names of mint officials, local governors or simply private individuals.

A number of the other coin types from the Artemision may also have been issued by the Lydians, but the wide variety of designs encountered points to other sources as well. Two pieces with a seal's head design are assumed to be from Phocaea, the seal being the usual badge of this city because of its name ($\phi\omega\kappa\eta$ = 'seal'), and indeed larger pieces depict the seal accompanied by the letter phi (**8**); a type with a recumbent lion (**9**) is linked with Miletus through comparison with later issues of the city; and a type with a griffin's head might have originated in Teos or, again, Phocaea. One particularly interesting variety which depicts the forepart of a stag (**10**) has been identified as a fractional piece of the most famous early inscribed coin, the electrum stater with a grazing stag type and the phrase 'I am the badge of Phanes' in Ionic letters inscribed retrograde (**11**). The identity of this Phanes has not yet been established. The stag is the beast of Artemis, which is fitting for the temple at Ephesus, but the inscription excludes the coin being an official issue of that city. The only recorded historical Phanes was a mercenary leader from Halicarnassus, (where one example of this coin is known to have been acquired in modern times). This Phanes was fighting in Egypt in the 530s and so he seems too late in date to have been connected with these coins, but since his grandfather probably had the same name and would have been alive in the early sixth century it is possible that Halicarnassus was the city of origin.

The Artemision finds did not contain examples of all the early electrum coinages of Asia Minor. The island of Samos had its own series, struck to a weight standard not represented at Ephesus. These Samian electrum coins are characterised by their weight, by the form of their reverse punch marks and by their obverse types, which developed from a jumbled pattern of marks to vaguely recognizable animal forms, including the facing lion's head (**12**) which later became the familiar badge of Samos. The attribution of these coins to Samos is confirmed by the evidence of finds from the island, including an important hoard discovered in the late nineteenth century. An interesting anecdote that confirms the attribution of coinage at Samos at an early date describes how Polycrates, the local tyrant, deceived the Spartans, who were besieging Samos in 525/4 BC, by paying them off with lead coins coated with gold (*Herodotus* 3, 56). For 'gold' we should understand 'electrum' because, although none of the known Samian electrum coins have been dated as late as Polycrates, it is the island's early electrum coinage that is no doubt behind this story.

One of the most noticeable features of the early electrum coinages of Asia Minor is the high proportion of very small, fractional pieces issued. The three weight systems apparently in use were based on staters weighing respectively 17.2 grammes (the 'Euboeic', e.g. at Samos), 16.1 grammes (the 'Phocaic', e.g. at Phocaea) and 14.1 grammes (the 'Milesian', e.g. in Lydia and southern Ionia), but the commonest pieces are fractions such as thirds, sixths and, in the case of the 'Milesian' fractions, a great range of smaller denominations down to a ninety-sixth. This last coin was a minute piece weighing as little as a tenth of a gramme. The production of such a wide range of small pieces suggests that these coins were used in a society where monetary values were reckoned with great precision. They would have provided for payments of many kinds, including relatively small payments, though even the smallest coin was worth a day's subsistence and would still have been too valuable for everyday marketplace purchases. The tiniest pieces must have been very awkward to handle; they were surely not meant to circulate very actively or travel far. Indeed, most of these earliest coinages must essentially have been for local use only.

It has been noted that some, at least, of the early electrum coinages can be attributed to cities, such as Sardes (for the Lydian kingdom), Miletus and Phocaea, although no name of a city or ethnic of a people is inscribed upon them. The only recognizable inscriptions are the names of persons. It is therefore to be envisaged that individuals may have authorised issues of coinage, either in an official capacity as local rulers or governors, or as private persons, for example merchants. In later periods the authority to issue coinage was invariably reserved for the State, but the variety of types, as well as the occasional appearance of a personal name, has tempted scholars to suggest that many of the early electrum coin designs must have been the personal seals of individuals rather than of cities. This may have been so, especially in the earliest phases, but it is also possible that the cities still authorised these coinages but allowed the individuals responsible for production to decorate them with types of their own choice, which would of course have changed with each official until, in time, it was decided to settle on a definitive design by which the city's coinage would more easily be recognized.

The intrinsic value of early electrum coins varies considerably according to the ratio of gold to silver present in the alloy. Nevertheless, these coins were issued in carefully weighed units and with a stamp which must have given them an officially fixed value so that they could be paid out in return for services or goods at an agreed rate. Obviously, the electrum pieces with a lower proportion of gold in the alloy were worth less in real terms than the pieces of similar weight, and therefore the same nominal value, containing more gold. There were profits to be made in issuing overvalued electrum coins and, in fact, the overvaluation of struck metal as currency may have been one of the main reasons for the invention of coinage in the first place. But the uncertain real value of the early electrum coins probably restricted their usage and it is not surprising that in time a coinage of separate gold and silver issues developed. Once this began to happen, apparently around the middle of the sixth century BC, the electrum coinages were very quickly replaced by new silver issues which had a more exact worth and, in their smaller fractional denominations, provided a flexible range of values that extended far below that of the electrum.

CHAPTER 3

The development to East and West (c.550-475 BC)

The first gold and silver coins

King Croesus of Lydia (c.560-547 BC) has been credited with issuing the first gold and silver coins. Croesus was, of course, a man of legendary wealth, well known to the Greeks of his time. It is not surprising, therefore, that a tradition should have grown up which links the name of Croesus with the development from electrum to gold and silver coinage. There was in antiquity a gold coin known as a 'Croeseid' and it is assumed that this must be the well known piece which depicts on its obverse confronting lion and bull foreparts, as this seems to be the earliest identifiable gold coin (**13**). This type appears on both gold and silver (**14**) coins and these are seen as the successors to the earlier Lydian issues in electrum with the lion's head in profile. However, evidence from hoards increasingly suggests that few, if any, of these 'Croeseids' could have been issued before the fall of the Lydian kingdom to the Persians in 547BC.

There are no other gold coins that can be dated as early as the lion and bull 'Croeseids', but there are silver coinages that some believe to be as early as, if not earlier than, the 'Croeseid' series. Because of the tradition linking King Pheidon of Argos with coinage at Aegina, the first Aeginetan silver issues have often been regarded as possibly the earliest of all silver coins, but the evidence of hoards has confirmed that no Aeginetan, nor any other, silver coins can be dated as early as the time of Pheidon. The hoards point to a date after 550 BC for the earliest issues of Aegina and the same can be said of the other notable early Greek silver coinages, from Athens and Corinth.

Conclusive evidence for the date and identity of the very first silver coinage, like that of the earliest electrum, remains to be found; but there is no doubting the importance of the technological developments that must have facilitated production of the new coinages in silver. In the second half of the sixth century BC almost all the minting cities of western Asia Minor were converted to the exclusive use of silver coin, and the new form of currency also spread rapidly overseas at this time, to the Greek mainland and, soon afterwards, to the Greek colonies in southern Italy, Sicily and elsewhere in the Mediterranean. Abundant supplies of silver bullion were needed to feed these new coinages so there must have been a great increase in the mining and refining of silver ores. For some reason production of gold coinage did not expand alongside that of silver. The only producers of gold coinage seem to have been the Persian authorities now in charge in Lydia. A few cities in Asia Minor, notably Cyzicus and Phocaea and the island of Lesbos, clung to the use of electrum coinage long after it had virtually disappeared elsewhere, and rare examples of electrum are found alongside the earliest issues of silver coinage from Athens and northern Greece and also from western Asia Minor, again in the period of the Ionian Revolt against Persia (499–494 BC); but these electrum issues are altogether insignificant when compared with the output of silver. From about 550 to 475 BC, that is from the first use of silver coinage to just after the famous wars between the Greeks and the Persians, there was a remarkable expansion in the production and usage of coined money, and in this period it was unquestionably the silver coin that reigned supreme.

The spread of silver coinage at this time was closely related to the pattern of settlement of Greek-speaking peoples living mostly in the city states which made up what we now refer to as the 'Greek world' in the sixth century BC. Greeks had been leaving their homelands to establish colonies throughout the Mediterranean and beyond since around the beginning of the milennium. Western Asia Minor, the north Aegean, the Black Sea coasts, parts of the western Mediterranean, notably southern Italy and Sicily, and Cyrenaica (Libya) in north Africa had all been settled. The colonies were widely scattered and often far from their mother cities, but strong links were retained with the homelands and settlements often kept in close contact with each other, particularly ones founded by Greeks from the same region or sharing the same dialect (for example Achaean, Aeolian, Dorian, Ionian). It is therefore not surprising that a successful new invention was able to make rapid progress over such a wide area.

The dates and chronologies and even, in some cases, the identities of the many coinages which emerged during this period of expansion are occasionally difficult to determine. Inscriptions on the coins are rare, names of dateable rulers are virtually non-existent, and other historical or archaeological evidence which might help to place them is scanty and often ambiguous. We are left largely with the evidence of the coins themselves. Physical features, such as fabric, weight and design, can be looked at; comparisons can be drawn between different groups of apparently contemporary coins and links can be proposed between these early coins and later, more firmly attributed and dated issues. Information on the circumstances and locations of finds is also important, when it exists and if it is reliable. Hoards of coins, concealed for reasons of safety in antiquity but never recovered by their original owners, can be particularly useful, especially ones that contain a mixture of coins from different sources. In such hoards contemporary groupings of coins can sometimes be seen clearly and a picture of the overall pattern of chronological development emerges. Occasionally a date can be brought in and groups of coins can be attached to it, but so-called 'fixed points' sometimes come under attack from new, conflicting evidence or from a reassessment of old evidence. Thus, the chronologies and in some cases the attributions of these early Greek coinages must be regarded as somewhat flexible.

The East

Because of the very wide geographical distribution of coinages in this period and because of the uncertain chronological relationships between the coins of different regions it is simplest to look at each area separately. We may start with Asia Minor, as this was the birthplace of the earlier electrum coinages. Hoard evidence indicates that the earliest silver coinages, beginning in the period 550-525 BC, were the 'Croeseids' from Sardes (**14**) and certain issues from Caria to the south-west, which have as their obverse type the forepart of a snarling lion (**20**). The coins of both these series have a dumpy fabric and generally ovoid or irregular shape similar to the early electrum issues, and their reverses show striking by two separate punches, another early feature. A recently discovered hoard from southern Turkey includes large numbers of both these coinages and most noticeable is the high proportion of very small fractions present (**21**). It has been remarked that fractional denominations of the 'Croeseids' seem much rarer than the stater, or double siglos, which weighs about 10.8 grammes and its half piece, the siglos, but this new hoard indicates that this is not the case.

Another silver coinage with a distinctly 'early' fabric is a series that has a selection of obverse designs, including horse forepart (**22**), crab, sphinx, and two dolphins, coupled with a reverse comprising one large square punch and one small punch, which again resembles some of the early electrum issues. Coins of this group, which were struck to a weight standard, with a stater of 12.2 grammes, which is known as the 'Aeginetic', have been found in hoards dated to the late sixth century BC from the Cyclades. It is thought that they may have been produced either in the Aegean islands or in one or more of the coastal cities of western Asia Minor. Further south a group of cities on the islands off the coast of south-west Asia Minor, including Camirus (23) and Lindos on Rhodes and Poseidium on Carpathos, issued early silver coins which have different obverse types particular to each city but a shared reverse form which is again quite distinctive. It comprises two rectangular, patterned depressions separated by a broad band. A similar effect is visible on the reverses of some of the lion forepart staters from Caria on the mainland nearby. Yet another variety of reverse was used on the earliest silver coinage that has been attributed to the region of Lycia, east of Caria. Stater-size pieces have a lion's head obverse type coupled with a reverse that shows a 'Union Jack' pattern of bold crossed lines within a single square punch (24).

Many other city-states in Asia Minor were producing silver coins by the end of the sixth century. The island of Chios began issuing its extensive series of two-drachma pieces, weighing about 7.8 grammes. The obverse type depicts a seated sphinx (25). This was the badge of Chios; it remained as the identifying emblem on the coinage of the island for centuries to come and is found on the official weights used by every trader in the island (*see* **Fig. 4**). The reverse of the coin shows a simple square incuse divided into four quarters. Usage of this form of punch was widespread at this time; it is found on many other coins from Asia Minor, particularly in Ionia, and also in the Aegean islands and north Greece. In the north of Asia Minor another island producing early silver coinage with a simple reverse punch was Lesbos (26). The early coins of Lesbos are interesting because of two unusual characteristics. Firstly, the punch is unusually small in comparison with the surface area of the coin face; and secondly, the coins are of base silver, whereas Greek silver coins of the early periods are almost invariably very fine. One of the commonest early silver coins from Asia Minor was produced by the important city of Miletus in Ionia. Staters weighing about 12 grammes were issued (though the attribution of these coins to Miletus has been disputed), but the piece most frequently encountered is a small coin, usually classed as a diobol, weighing only about 1.2 grammes (27). This was also one of the earliest coins to be struck with a fully designed reverse die. The design on the reverse is a stylised, star-shaped, floral pattern, while on the obverse a lion's head once again appears.

The variations in fabric, technique and weight standards revealed by the coinages of Asia Minor in the late sixth century BC suggest that a certain amount of separate, independent development in coining practices was taking place. During this period most of the region came under the control of the Persian Empire, but the Persian advance seems to

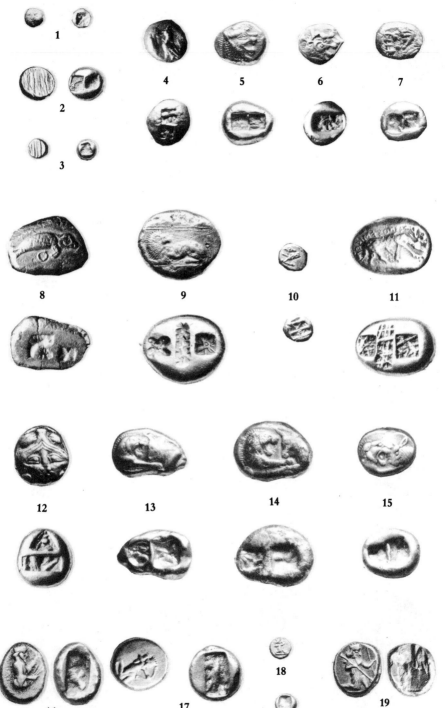

PLATE 1 Archaic Asia Minor

PLATE 2 Archaic Caria, Lycia, Aegean Islands

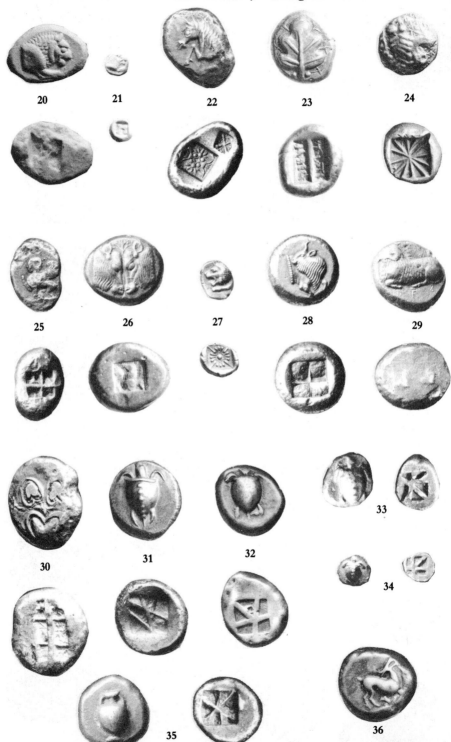

20 21 22 23 24

25 26 27 28 29

30 31 32 33 34

35 36

PLATE 3   Archaic Greece, Macedonia

PLATE 4   Archaic Macedonia, south Italy

51

52

53

54

55

56

57

58

59

60

61

PLATE 5 Archaic Sicily

62   63   64   65

66   67   68   69

66   67   68   69

71

70

PLATE 6   Classical Sicily

72

73

74

75

76

78

79

80

77

81

82

83

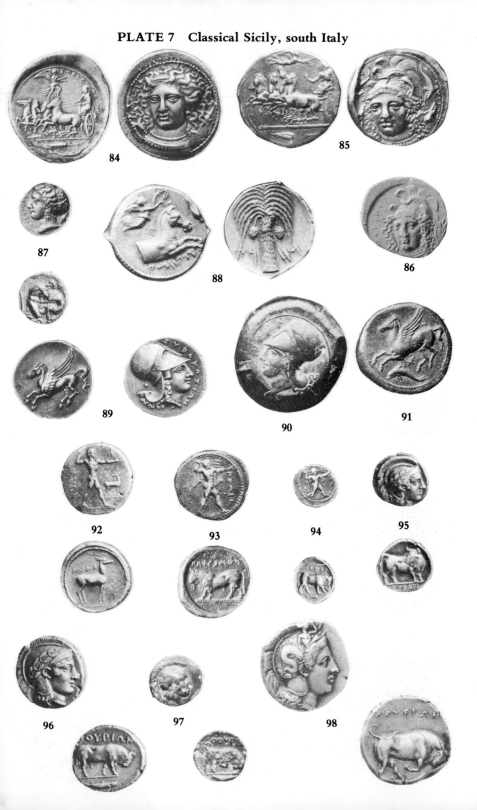

PLATE 7   Classical Sicily, south Italy

84

85

87

88

86

89

90

91

92

93

94

95

96

97

98

PLATE 8   Classical south Italy, Spain, Gaul, Athens

99

100

102

101

103

104

105

106

103

107

108

109

110

111

112

113

114

115

have had little effect initially on the coinages of the city states. Then, in 499 BC, the Greek cities of Ionia and other Asiatic Greeks rebelled against their Persian overlords and a series of rare electrum coins, showing a variety of obverse types but a uniform style and fabric, has been attributed to the Revolt. The coins are stater-size pieces, struck to the old 'Milesian' standard used in the earlier electrum period, weighing just over 14 grammes. The obverse types suggest identifications with various cities, such as Chios and Samos (**28**), though it is also thought that the entire series could have been struck at a single mint. A number of issues of silver fractions have also been associated with the Revolt. However, after the collapse of the rebellion, in 494 BC, there seems to have been a general curtailment of minting activity in western Asia Minor and many cities did not resume production until after the Persian Wars ended in the 470s.

Fig. 4 *One-mina weight of Chios*

Two other notable centres of coinage production within the Persian Empire were the island of Cyprus and the country of Cyrenaica in north Africa. Both these regions had been absorbed into the Empire under Cambyses in 525 BC, but they subsequently developed coinages that are essentially Greek in character. Cyprus in the sixth century contained several small kingdoms ruling over a mixed population of Greek or Phoenician origin. Production of silver coinage seems to have begun late in the sixth century and the wide variety of early-style issues, represented in large numbers in hoards from Cyprus and Egypt, indicates that many separate mints were probably operating on the island by the early fifth century. The earliest issues are difficult to attribute, though one group can be assigned to Salamis because its coins are inscribed with the name of King Euelthon (*c.*560-525 BC), founder of the dynasty which ruled the city. Hoard evidence suggests that the 'Euelthon' coinage probably did not begin until after the king's death. The name is accompanied by a recumbent ram as the obverse type; the reverse is notable for being completely smooth (**29**). Other early coinages from Cyprus have been attributed to the cities of Lapethus, Paphos and Idalium. Most of the Cypriot issues have a stater which weighs about 11 grammes and is equivalent to a double siglos on the Persian weight standard. Fractional pieces are also not uncommon.

Cyrenaica was first settled by Greeks in the seventh century BC when the city of Cyrene was founded by colonists from the island of Thera, and in the sixth century other cities were founded as more settlers arrived from the Aegean islands and the Peloponnese. Production of coinage began towards the end of the sixth century, perhaps in the reign of Battus IV (510–470 BC), king of the native dynasty which ruled the country at this time on behalf of the Persians. The silphium plant, which grew only in Cyrenaica and was famed in antiquity for its healing powers, was adopted from the start as the identifying badge on Cyrenaican coins. The very first issues (**30**) show the fruit of the silphium on the obverse. On the reverse are two rectangular punch marks side by side which, together with the dumpy fabric, give these coins an appearance very similar to some of the early silver issues from western Asia Minor (e.g. Camirus and Lindos on Rhodes). The silphium fruits were soon replaced by a design depicting the whole plant, then, from about 500 BC, the reverse also gained a pictorial type; a wide variety of designs were used, including the head of Zeus Ammon, which later became the standard partner of the silphium plant on Cyrenaican coinage. As well as Cyrene itself, the city of Barce and perhaps other cities in the area, made issues of coins.

In western Asia Minor a coinage was now being produced which is usually referred to as the 'regal' coinage of the Persian Empire. The Achaemenid authorities at the former Lydian capital of Sardes had continued to issue 'Croeseid' coins (**15**) until, during the reign of Darius I (521–485 BC), the lion and bull design was replaced with a new type depicting a crowned figure. The new coins were struck in both gold and silver with the same fabric and on the same weight standard as the 'Croeseids'. The gold piece, which came to be known as the daric, weighed 8.3 grammes; the silver siglos weighed about 5.4 grammes and could be exchanged with the gold daric at the rate of 20 : 1. Fractions in either metal are exceedingly rare. The crowned figure on the obverse, which has usually been interpreted as a stylised representation of the Persian Great King, has four different forms, three of which (**16, 17, 19**) were used early in the fifth century. The first type, which is confined to an issue of silver sigloi, shows the king half-length, holding a bow and arrows (**16**). The second type, which appears on darics (**17**), sigloi and fractions (**18**) in both gold and silver, has the king kneeling, drawing the bow. This type brings to mind Herodotus's story of the actions of Darius upon hearing that a people known as the Athenians had helped burn down Sardes during the Ionian Revolt. He is alleged to have called for a bow and, firing an arrow into the sky, sworn to punish these people, whose name had to be repeated to him three times a day so that he would not forget them (*Herodotus* 5, 105). These first two coin types have been found in hoards with 'Croeseids'; they are certainly the earliest, and also the rarest, of the series. They were succeeded, perhaps in the 480s, by the third type which depicts the king running, holding a bow and spear (**19**). Finds of coin hoards indicate that huge quantities of Persian sigloi were produced in the fifth century, and many may belong to the period covered by the campaigns of Darius and his successor Xerxes against the Greeks in 490 and 480-79 BC, when the Persian military commanders would have needed plenty of silver in a convenient form for their expenses.

The darics and sigloi were recognized as the 'imperial' coins of the Persians (at least by Greeks), but they were restricted to the most western satrapies (provinces) of the empire in Asia Minor. They were not produced for circulation in the central or eastern parts of the empire because these areas did not use coinage as money; instead, the people there continued to weigh precious metals as currency. However, sigloi and other coins from the 'Greek' world, especially in silver, did travel to these areas, where they were then used as bullion, often cut into pieces or melted down. Many important mixed hoards of early Greek silver coins have been found in the East, particularly in Egypt, and these have provided valuable information for working out the chronologies of these early issues. The most significant eastern hoard of recent years was discovered in Egypt in 1969. Now known as the Asyut hoard, it is thought to have been buried around 475 BC, or possibly a little later, and it contained some nine hundred silver coins from over seventy different mints or cities. The hoard included coins originating from areas within the Persian Empire, but the great majority of the coins had travelled from much further west. It would be appropriate now for us to turn westwards and return to the Aegean where, using the evidence of the Asyut and other hoards, we may resume our survey of the development of early silver coinage in other areas of the Greek world.

The Aegean islands and Greece

Two hoards found in the nineteenth century, one on Thera and one on another island in the Cyclades, are crucial for our understanding of the early coinage of the Aegean. In these hoards were coins belonging to the group already mentioned that might have been produced either in the islands or in the coastlands of Asia Minor, together with early silver coins

Fig. 5   *Principal minting cities in the Archaic period: the Aegean*

that can certainly be attributed to the Cyclades, also many coins from Aegina, off the coast of the Peloponnese, and some staters of Miletus, which thus provide a link between the island coinages and the early silver issues of Asia Minor.

The coins of Aegina are by far the most numerous in these two hoards, and it is clear from the evidence of other hoards as well that Aegina was not just the most important of the island mints but was one of the most important and influential coin producers in the Greek world at this time. Aegina began minting silver coins early, within the period 550-525 BC, and the high output and wide distribution of early Aeginetan silver coins is illustrated by their frequency in all the earliest hoards from Egypt and elsewhere in the East. The archaic Aeginetan coins have a sea turtle on the obverse and on the reverse is the mark of a punch which began as a rough square incuse, then developed into a design, first of a 'Union Jack' arrangement of crossed lines (**31**) and then into a 'skew' pattern of five segments separated by crossed bands (**32**).

The two-drachma stater of Aegina weighed 12.2 grammes and this weight standard was adopted widely in the Aegean islands, in mainland Greece and in Asia Minor. The islands of the Cyclades were unusually active in producing coins in this early period compared with later times. Most of the islands employed the Aeginetic weight standard and their coins also have a similar fabric to the early issues of Aegina. The coins of each island are distinguished by their use of different obverse types, such as the amphora for Andros, (**35**), wine kantharos for Naxos, goat for

Paros (**36**), eagle for Siphnos and dolphins for Thera.

On the Greek mainland, Athens was one of the first city-states to strike silver coins. The earliest Athenian coins, which began within the period 550-525 BC, are known by the German term *Wappenmünzen*, meaning 'heraldic coins', because one of the theories put forward to explain the wide variety of obverse designs (amphora, Gorgon head (**37**), triskeles, wheel, and so on) is that they represent the heraldic emblems of the individuals responsible for production of each issue. The commonest denomination of the *Wappenmünzen* is the two-drachma piece, or didrachm, weighing about 8.6 grammes; but many fractional pieces were also issued.

Towards the end of the sixth century the *Wappenmünzen* series ended and was replaced by a new coinage (**38-9**) which, unlike its predecessor, stated its Athenian origins explicitly. The obverse depicted a helmeted head of Athena and on the reverse was an owl, together with the abbreviated name of the city: AΘE. This combination of types was to remain on the coinage of Athens for centuries to come and the coins themselves came to be known by the name 'Owls'. Owls from the period down to about 480 BC, which are often referred to as 'archaic owls', were issued in enormous quantities, and mostly in the form of tetradrachms (four-drachma pieces) weighing 17.2 grammes (**38**). They also travelled far and are found in large numbers, particularly in hoards from within the Persian Empire (the Asyut hoard, for instance, contained one hundred and sixty three specimens). The main reason for this outpouring of silver coin from Athens, which contrasts sharply with the much more limited output and localised circulation of the *Wappenmünzen*, is that Athens was by now exploiting the rich deposits of silver in her mines at Laurium in Attica. In 483 BC it was reported that the State treasury held a hundred talents of silver from the Attic mines. This would have been sufficient to strike a hundred and fifty thousand new tetradrachms. With such enormous riches to hand it was proposed that a donation could be given to every citizen (*Herodotus* 7, 144), but instead the more prudent advice of Themistocles was followed and it was decided that the money should be spent on rebuilding the Athenian navy which, of course, was subsequently victorious against the Persian fleet at the great sea battle of Salamis in 480 BC.

On the large island of Euboea, close to Attica, the cities of Chalcis, Eretria and Carystus all produced silver coins as early as the third quarter of the sixth century BC. As at Athens, the earliest coins, which have been found in hoards alongside Athenian *Wappenmünzen*, have designs on one side only, but before long types were employed on both obverse and reverse. The principal types used on Euboean coins in this early period were: flying eagle (Chalcis), cow obverse with octopus reverse (Eretria) and cow obverse with cock reverse (**40**: Carystus).

Elsewhere in central Greece coinage did not begin until towards the end of the sixth century BC. The cities of Boeotia, which had formed a League under the leadership of Thebes, all used the same design on the obverse of their coins. This was an oval convex shield with a curved opening on either side. The standard coin of the Boeotian League was the didrachm on the Aeginetic weight standard, weighing about 6 grammes (**41**). This weight standard was also used in Phocis, where the cities also formed a federation and shared a single coinage, which was struck mostly in the smaller denominations of hemidrachm (half-drachma) and obol.

The first coins of the Corinthians date from within the same period (*c*.550-525 BC) as those of their great trading rivals, the Athenians and Aeginetans. The earliest Corinthian coins are, however, noticeably flatter (**42-3**) in appearance than most other early coins, suggesting perhaps that the Corinthians developed minting techniques independent of their contemporaries. The obverse type was the winged horse, Pegasus, which was, according to legend, tamed by Bellerophon at Corinth. It was accompanied by the archaic letter *koppa*, the city's initial. The punch design on the reverse developed from a 'Union Jack' to a 'swastica' pattern, and then, in about 500 BC, was replaced by a head of Athena within an incuse square. The standard Corinthian coin (**42**) was the stater of three drachmae weighing 8.6 grammes, a weight standard equivalent to half an Athenian tetradrachm.

In western Greece, where the influence of Corinth was usually dominant, coinage began on the island of Corcyra (Corfu) in the late sixth century BC. Silver coins (**46**) were issued on a local weight standard with an obverse type depicting a cow and calf and a reverse design composed of two rectangular punches, or later panels, containing patterns. The only other mint in the region in this period was that of Corinth's colony Leucas, which began issuing silver staters on the Corinthian model in the 480s.

North Greece

In this early period the area to the north of the Aegean Sea was one of the most important for the production of silver coinage. There were rich deposits of silver ores both in Macedonia, in the western half of the region, and in Thrace to the east, and perhaps richest of all was the area of Mount Pangaeus on the border between them. These silver resources were exploited by all the inhabitants of the region: the cities of Greek colonists on the coasts and islands; the semi-Greek rulers of the kingdom of Macedonia; and the Macedonian and Thracian tribes of the interior.

Large denomination coins, such as the eight-drachma piece (octadrachm) were produced as normal units of currency, and the frequency with which the coins of this region occur in eastern hoards, especially from Egypt, gives a clear indication that silver was an important export commodity in trade between this region and the east. It is worth noting that output from the region as a whole seems to have been at its peak around 500 BC and shortly after, when these northern Greek lands were under Persian control.

The date of the first issues of coinage from Macedonia or Thrace is uncertain, but once again useful evidence is provided by the Egyptian hoards and these indicate that some series must have begun about 525 BC or shortly afterwards. In Macedonia the cities of the three-pronged peninsula of Chalcidice, which gained its name from the Euboean settlers who had been the major colonisers of the area, possibly learned the practice of coinage from their mother cities, as they all adopted for their coinage the Euboean weight standard, with a stater of 17.2 grammes. The city of Dicaea (Macedonia) also copied the coin types of its mother city, Eretria, but most of the mints adopted their own designs and as a result the area yields a wide variety of attractive and interesting coin types. The most visually exciting types are compositions depicting a lion attacking different beasts: a boar at Stagira, a stag at Scione and a bull at Acanthus (**47**). It is tempting to associate these designs with the spread of Persian influence in the area, because lion themes are particularly common in the art of the Near East.

Further east, the Greek cities and islands off the coast of Thrace first began minting silver coins in about 525 BC. One of the earliest producers was the city of Abdera, founded in 546 BC by refugees from Teos, on the Ionian coast of Asia Minor. The Teians who colonised Abdera should have been familiar with coinage, since the earliest electrum issues had circulated in Ionia, but the Abderites did not begin to mint their own coins until later in the century. However, continuing contact with the mother city is clearly shown by the fact that the same type, of a griffin, was selected for the first silver issues of both cities but, while at Teos the griffin always faced right, at Abdera it always faced left (**48**). The reverses of the early coins of Abdera have a simple punch mark divided into quarters, which is a form of reverse particularly common in the north Aegean area as a whole in this period. Most of Abdera's considerable output of early silver coinage was minted in the large denominations of tetradrachm and octadrachm, struck to a local weight standard. Somewhat smaller and lighter are the early silver coins attributed to the island of Thasos (**49**). These are staters, weighing about 9.8 grammes and having a lively obverse design depicting a satyr carrying off a nymph.

In the Thraco-Macedonian region the Greek cities were confined to the coasts and islands; in the interior lived tribes of semi-Greek or non-Greek peoples. In the west was the kingdom of Macedonia with its capital at Aegae. At the start of the fifth century BC the city of Aegae began issuing a series of silver coins (**50**) which have a goat, as the city's emblem, on the obverse and a simple quartered punch mark on the reverse. The first king of Macedon to sign coins was Alexander I, who reigned from about 498 to 451 BC, though the coins bearing his name did not start appearing until about 480 BC. Under Alexander octadrachms (**116**), tetradrachms and smaller denominations were all produced with various equestrian types apparently signifying the different denominations.

Some of the tribes which shared the lands north of the Aegean with the Macedonians are known only from their coins. For others we have information on their general location from literary sources, but little else is known of them. Yet these obscure peoples produced, in only a short space of time, some of the more interesting coinages of this early period. They are particularly noted for their large denomination silver coins, such as octadrachms, which were produced plentifully and which are again found in large numbers in eastern hoards, so that it has been possible to work out approximate dates for the various issues.

On the tribal coins the usual quartered punch reverse is accompanied by a variety of obverse types. These obverses can be divided into two main groups. The first consists of designs with animals, usually cattle or horses. The Derrones, a tribe that may have inhabited Paeonia (southern Yugoslavia), issued twelve-drachma pieces (**51**) with designs depicting oxen, sometimes pulling a cart, accompanied by various figures including, possibly, the gods Ares and Hermes. The Ichnae, and later the Edoni, who occupied the region to the east of the River Strymon, also produced issues with a herdsman, possibly Hermes, walking with two oxen (**53**). The Bisalti who, like the Edonia, did not begin striking coins until after 480 BC, issued octadrachms with a type depicting a huntsman, carrying two spears, standing beside a horse (**52**). This is similar to one of the designs on coins of Alexander I of Macedon. The second major group of obverse types comprises orgiastic designs. One of the earliest coinages of the Thraco-Macedonian region, which probably began about 525 BC, is a series depicting a nymph seducing a satyr (**54**). This type at first was struck on thick dumpy flans with a rough irregular square punch mark on the reverse; then, as the reverse developed into a regular quartered square, apparently around 500 BC, the fabric also became thinner and wider and the figures on the obverse became larger. These issues have been labelled 'Lete', but they were probably issued by a northern tribe from the region of Mount Pangaeus. The Orescii, who are known only from their coins, but who also probably inhabited the area of Mount Pangaeus, issued coins with an obverse type depicting a centaur carrying off a nymph (**55**). The same type appears also on coins signed by various other obscure peoples: Dionysioi, Letaioi, Pernaioi and Zaielioi, who were probably neighbours of the Orescii and who would also have shared an interest in the Dionysiac cult so obviously popular in these northern regions.

The West

Southern Italy and Sicily were first settled by Greeks in the eighth and seventh centuries BC, and in the later sixth century it was the inhabitants of the Greek cities founded by these colonists who produced the first coinages from the region.

The principal cities of southern Italy in the sixth century were Sybaris, Metapontum, Croton and Caulonia on the south coast, and Poseidonia and Velia on the west coast. Sybaris, Metapontum and Croton were all founded originally by Achaean settlers from the Peloponnese; Caulonia was founded by colonists from Croton, and Poseidonia was a colony of Sybaris. Standing apart from these 'Achaean' cities was Velia, which was founded in about 540 BC by refugees from Phocaea in Asia Minor. The important city of Rhegium, situated on the end of the 'toe' of south Italy, developed a coinage system which places it within the economic sphere of Sicily, so for the purposes of this account it will be treated, as it usually is, alongside the Sicilian mints.

The most remarkable feature of the early coinage issued by south Italy's Achaean cities and their colonies is the unusual experimental technique of manufacture, developed from repoussé work. This technique, which involved the striking of the same design in relief and in intaglio on a markedly thin flan, was peculiar to these cities. It required an accurate alignment of the two dies to allow the punch carved in relief to push the metal into the engraving on the anvil. Because this method of minting coins is so different from that practised by other cities in the Greek world it has been conjectured that the development of coinage in south Italy must have been largely independant of outside influences, possibly because it happened very early, before the region could have imported, and so become familiar with, coins from the eastern Mediterranean. It is presumed that the idea of coinage arrived from the Aegean, but the technique of production developed separately in one of the Achaean cities, from where it quickly spread to all the others. The theory that the technique might have been invented by Pythagoras, the great philosopher and mathematician who moved to Croton from his native Samos in 530 BC, is attractive but entirely speculative. Not only

Fig. 6   *South Italy and Sicily*

was the same technique adopted by all these cities, but also the same method of design, with the type enclosed within a patterned frame, and the same weight standard, known as the 'Achaean'. This weight standard has a silver stater of 8 grammes divided into thirds (drachmae) and sixths (triobols). No gold or electrum coinage was produced in southern Italy in this early period.

The date when coinage was first struck in southern Italy is difficult to determine, though it is possible to link together some of the early issues with coins from the eastern Mediterranean because of their appearance in mixed hoards such as the Asyut hoard and the great Taranto hoard (discovered in 1911) which, though buried in Italy, included a large quantity of coins that had earlier been put together in the East. The key date, around which the chronologies of all the early south Italian coinages tend to be based, is 510 BC, when the great city of Sybaris was destroyed by its neighbour Croton. It is presumed that the early incuse coinage of Sybaris must have been struck before this date, and thus the issues of the other Achaean cities which are closest in form to those of Sybaris must also predate this event. The incuse technique lasted until about 440 BC, and in the meantime, although the weights of the coins remained the same, the fabric changed from 'spread flan' to 'medium' to 'dumpy'. All the coins of Sybaris are 'spread flan'. This was therefore the sixth century form, beginning perhaps about 530 BC. The 'medium flan' was then introduced about 500 BC and it lasted until about 475 BC when it was replaced by the 'dumpy' issues.

Sybaris was a powerful and opulent city, whose people had a reputation for luxurious living that has given our language the word 'sybarite'. Because of its preeminence it is thought likely to have been the first city to strike coinage in southern Italy. The coins of Sybaris (**56**) have the type of a standing bull, looking back over its shoulder, together with the abbreviated name of the city in local letter forms. The bull of Sybaris also appears as the coin type at a number of other, lesser cities, which were either colonies of Sybaris or were otherwise under her influence, including Pyxus and Sirinos which produced a joint issue, and Laus. Some of these issues might have been produced by refugees from Sybaris following the destruction of the city in 510 BC.

The coinage of Metapontum outnumbers that of Sybaris in the earliest hoards of south Italian coinage. This was clearly another important mint. The type on the coinage of Metapontum is an ear of barley and, as is normally the case in south Italy, the city's name is recorded, usually in abbreviated form. From about 500 BC the flan size was reduced to 'medium' and in this phase a number of examples of overstriking of the Metapontine design on coins of other cities, notably Corinth (**57**) and Selinus in Sicily, have been recorded. Overstrikes such as these are important for linking together the chronologies of coinage issues from different cities and regions.

Croton and Caulonia probably began minting soon after Sybaris and Metapontum. Both used coin types relating to Apollo: a tripod at Croton (**58**) and a figure of the god at Caulonia. Croton produced a very large coinage which also contained more variations in design than are generally seen on the coins of the other south Italian cities in this period. A number of symbols were included alongside the standard tripod, and on some issues, which may have been struck at other cities under Croton's control, there appeared incuse reverse types that are completely different from the obverse design.

On the west coast, the city of Poseidonia adopted the incuse technique, and later also the weight standard, of the other Achaean cities, though its earliest issues were struck to a slightly lower weight standard with a stater of 7.5 grammes divided into two drachms, as opposed to three at the other cities. The coins (59) depict Poseidon, the city's patron deity, in a form very similar to the Apollo on the coins of Caulonia. It appears that they were all issued in the last quarter of the sixth century BC.

The earliest coinage produced by the Phocaean settlers at Velia is, not surprisingly, quite different from that of the other south Italian cities (60). Its weight standard, fabric and types, with an obverse of a lion devouring its prey and a plain incuse square punch reverse, are all derived from Asia Minor. Linked with Velia and also with another Phocaean colony, Massalia (Marseilles) in southern France, are groups of small archaic silver coins which are similar to contemporary fractional pieces produced in Asia Minor. These are known as 'Auriol' type coins (61), from the site in southern France where the greatest numbers have been found.

The overall impression of unity in coinage production given by most of the cities in south Italy through their shared technique and weight system is not repeated in neighbouring Sicily. Here the earliest silver coinages seem to have been produced by the three Chalcidian colonies of Naxos and Zancle on the west coast and Himera on the north coast, and by the city of Selinus in the south-west of the island. At each of the Chalcidian cities the 'Euboeic' weight standard, with a stater of 17.2 grammes divided into thirds and sixths, was at first used, but otherwise the coinages have little in common. At Naxos (62) fully developed designs were used on both sides of the coins: a head of Dionysus on the obverse and a bunch of grapes on the reverse. Zancle (63) used for its obverse type a representation of the city's famous sickle-shaped harbour, from which the city derived its name, enclosing a dolphin. On the reverse is a curious geometric pattern with a sea shell in the centre. Himera (64) on the other hand, employed a simple 'Union Jack' reverse punch, coupled with a cock obverse type as the identifying badge of the city. The city of Selinus, which struck didrachms weighing the same as Corinthian staters (65), employed for its obverse type the leaf of a kind of parsley ($\sigma\epsilon\lambda\iota\nu\sigma\nu$) which gave the city its name. The reverse had at first a 'Union Jack' punch, but later an incuse square containing the leaf from the obverse.

The first issues of coinage from these Sicilian cities cannot be dated with any degree of certainty, though it seems likely that they began about 525 BC. Their endings may be more securely dated. In the early years of the fifth century BC other Greek cities in Sicily began to increase in power and, under the rule of ambitious tyrants, their expansion brought to an end the independence and, perhaps, the first phase of coinage, at the Chalcidian cities. Coin issues had already been produced in Acragas, Gela and Syracuse before the 490s, but it was under the tyrants who ruled these cities and their territories from then until the 460s that their coinages became really significant.

Theron, ruler of Acragas, and his son-in-law Gelon, tyrant of Gela and later from 485 BC of Syracuse, did not sign their coins, though it is possible to identify the issues that must have been produced under their authority. In 480 BC Gelon led the Greek defence of Sicily against the invading Carthaginians and his celebrated victory at the battle of Himera is recognized as being just as significant for the western Greeks as the victories of Athens, Sparta and their allies over the Persians at Salamis and Plataea were for the Greeks of the Aegean region. According to the ancient Sicilian historian Diodorus, a special coin, called the Demareteion after Gelon's queen Demarete, was issued in 480/479 BC following the battle of Himera (*Diod.* 11, 26, 3). This coin has in the past been identified with a rare ten-drachma silver piece of Syracuse (despite Diodorus's claim that the Demareteion was a gold coin), which bears the usual designs for the city of chariot on the obverse and head of Arethusa, the local water nymph, on the reverse (**70**). The chronologies of many Sicilian coinages have been built around this date with the so-called 'Demareteion' used as a fixed point. However, in recent years this silver coin has, on the basis of hoard evidence, been down-dated by some fifteen or more years. The link with Diodorus's story has thus been broken and the chronologies of related coinages reassessed.

A more secure 'fixed point' is provided by the coinage of Zancle which, from 494 BC, was completely transformed when the city was captured by a party of refugees from Samos in Asia Minor (*Herodotus* 6). The Samians produced a series of coins at Zancle (**68**) with designs adapted from the coinage of their homeland. The obverse type is the lion scalp of Samos; the reverse depicts the prow of a Samian warship. The takeover of Zancle by the Samians had been organized by Anaxilas, tyrant of Rhegium, on the other side of the straits that separate Sicily from southern Italy. Anaxilas was the third of the great tyrants who held sway over Sicily in this period. Within a few years of the Samians' arrival in Zancle, however, Anaxilas turned on his former allies and expelled them from the city. He then settled Zancle with Messenians from the Peloponnese, renamed it Messana, and produced joint issues of coinage from the two cities, Rhegium (**69**) and Messana, with shared designs: lion scalp obverse (copied from the issues of the Samians) and calf's head reverse.

Coin hoards and chronology

In this outline account of the development of early silver coinage in the Greek world we have made frequent reference to the evidence provided by coin hoards. The following table has been constructed to illustrate how the chronologies of coinages from separate mints can be linked together through the survival of examples in hoards. The table includes most of the important mixed hoards which contain early Greek silver coins, arranged into geographical and chronological groups, since the composition of any particular hoard is obviously determined by its location as well as the date and circumstances of assembly and burial (approximate dates of burial for each hoard or group of hoards are noted at the head of each column). Not every mint represented in the hoards has been included in the table; only the more significant mints from each region.

Hoards included in **Table A** (references to *IGCH*, see *Further reading*):
1 Asia Minor: southern Turkey 1982, unpublished.
2 Islands: Cyclades? 1889, *IGCH* 6
              Santorin 1821, *IGCH* 7
3 Egypt: Demanhur 1900, *IGCH* 1637
          Sakha 1897, *IGCH* 1639
4 Italy: Taranto 1911, *IGCH* 1874
5 Sicily: Selinunte? 1888, *IGCH* 2059
          Lentini 1906, *IGCH* 2060
          Calatabiano 1946, *IGCH* 2061
6 Egypt: Delta 1887, *IGCH* 1638
          Fayum 1957, *IGCH* 1646
          Benha el Asl 1928, *IGCH* 1640
7 Asia Minor: southern Turkey 1960, *IGCH* 1177
8 Sicily: Gela 1956, *IGCH* 2066
9 Egypt: Asyut 1969, *IGCH* 1644
10 Asia Minor: Lycia 1984 'Decadrachm hoard', unpublished.

Table A: Hoards of early silver coins

	1 AM.	2 Is.	3 Eg.	4 It.	5 Si.	6 Eg.	7 AM.	8 Si.	9 Eg.	10 AM.
	520	500	500	500	500	490	480	480	475	460
Italy:										
Matapontum				x					x	
Sybaris				x						
Velia				x						
Croton				x					x	
Sicily:										
Acragas								x		
Gela								x		
Himera				x					x	
Naxos					x					
Zancle					x		x	x	x	
Selinus				x	x					
Syracuse								x		
Greece:										
Thraco-Macedonian tribes			x	x		x			x	x
Bisalti										x
Thasos			x	x		x			x	x
Abdera			x			x	x		x	x
Macedonian kings									x	
Acanthus			x			x	x	x	x	x
Mende			x			x			x	x
Còrcyra			x						x	
Boeotia									x	
Euboea		x				x			x	x
Athens: "Wappenmünzen"		x	x			x			x	
early Owls			x			x	x	x	x	x
Aegina	x		x	x		x	x		x	
Corinth: early			x	x			x		x	
Athena head				x					x	
Melos									x	x
Naxos		x	x	x		x			x	
Paros		x	x						x	x
Asia Minor:										
Miletus	?	x	x						x	x
Teos			x						x	
Chios		x	x	x		x	x		x	x
Samos			x						x	x
Caria	x		x						x	x
Rhodes			x						x	x
Croeseids	x		x							
Persian sigloi							x		x	
Lycia	?		x			x			x	x
Cyprus			x			x			x	
Cyrenaica			x	x					x	

CHAPTER 4

Production and design

In the ancient Greek world coinage production did not follow any particular pattern. Some city-states and kingdoms issued coins on a regular, apparently systematic basis; in other places issues appeared only intermittently; in others again, notably Sparta in the classical period, coinage was not produced at all. Two principal factors were involved in the production and issue of coinage. Firstly, the raw materials and technology necessary for the manufacture of coinage had to be available. Secondly, the prospective coin issuers had to make the positive decision that they needed coinage, as opposed to some other form of currency; in other words there had to exist a demand for coinage.

Sources of bullion

Since most Greek coins, and indeed all the coins issued before the later fifth century BC, were struck in silver, gold or electrum, it is obvious that the ancient coinage producers above all needed access to supplies of precious metals. The mining of precious metals in the ancient world goes back in time long before the invention of coinage because of the need to supply the age-old demand for silver and gold, which had circulated in trade before coinage, often in the form of bullion ingots. Once coinage was invented there was a tendency for regions that had plentiful mineral resources to convert their precious metals into coinage. This was only natural; as well as the domestic needs for currency in states which had taken up the use of coined money there was also the international trade in precious metals which could now be supplied in the convenient form of coinage. We should therefore not be suprised that many of the most prolific coin producers were states with direct access to natural sources of the appropriate minerals.

In the earliest days of coinage the Lydians were able to produce issues in electrum because the River Pactolus, which flowed through the Lydian kingdom, carried alluvial deposits of mixed gold and silver originating from the area of Mount Tmolus. The Lydians may at one time have used a method of recovering the natural electrum reported by the ancient writer Strabo (11, 2, 19), who describes how a people from Asia Minor known as the Soanes trapped gold-bearing ores from their river in submerged greasy sheepskins. This practise of using sheepskins for collecting alluvial gold may be the origin of the legend of Jason and the Golden Fleece.

Another, more widespread method of obtaining mineral ores was underground mining. The most famous mine workings in ancient Greece were the Athenians' silver mines at Laurium in Attica. It was the intense exploitation of the mineral deposits beneath Laurium that enabled the Athenians to issue 'owls' in such huge quantities in the early fifth century BC. Other areas in the ancient Greek world famous for their mines included the island of Siphnos in the Aegean (gold and silver), various parts of the Macedonia-Thrace region, notably the mines of Philippi (formerly Krenides) exploited for their gold by Philip II of Macedon, Lampsacus (gold) and various other sites in Asia Minor, and Spain, whose immense resources of both gold and silver were exploited in turn by Phoenicians, Greeks, Carthaginians and Romans.

To the Greek city-states the importance of their mines is clear from the fact that they always tended to hold them in state ownership. The Thasians in the northern Aegean owned not only the mines on their own island but also those in their territories on the Thracian mainland opposite. The Thasians' gold mines on the mainland produced an average annual yield of eighty talents, forty per cent of Thasos's annual income (*Herodotus* 6, 46-7).

Our knowledge of mining in the Greek world is increasing all the time. The information comes from ancient sources, mainly literary, and also from the archaeological evidence yielded by the mining sites. Modern scientific methods of analysis can now provide the evidence for identifying the likely sources of silver for certain coinage issues, particularly in the earliest periods. This can be investigated by comparing the results of detailed analyses of both deposits from ancient mines and surviving coins. Studies of this kind have provided confirmation that the silver used to strike most of the earliest Athenian coinage, with the *Wappenmünzen* types, did not come from nearby Laurium, but from different sources; whereas the early 'owls' were certainly produced from Laurium silver.

In addition to the metals extracted from mineral ores there was always a certain amount of precious metal available in circulation, already refined. It existed in various forms, such as bullion, plate and jewellery and, of course, once coinage had been invented, in the coin issues already in circulation. Some Greek city-states managed to be major coin producers even though they did not have direct access to mineral deposits. Aegina, for instance, had no silver of its own. The Aeginetans presumably had to obtain through trade the large quantities of silver necessary for their impressive output of early silver coinage. The Greek cities of Sicily also had to import the silver they turned into coinage.

In the fifth century the Athenians were usually able to use bullion refined from their own silver mines at Laurium, together with the silver they exacted in tribute from their allies; in 431 BC Athens took an average revenue of six hundred talents in tribute, while the treasury on the Acropolis contained six thousand talents of coined silver and the city could also draw on a total of five hundred talents worth of uncoined gold and silver (*Thucydides* 2, 13, 3-5). However, in one well-documented period of crisis the Athenians had to resort to desperate measures to maintain their output of coinage. In 407/6 BC, during the Peloponnesian War, the Spartans were in occupation of Laurium and Athens's allies had revolted, so both of the main sources of silver usually available to Athens had been cut off. The city was fast running out of silver supplies so it was decided to issue a gold coinage (**113**) produced from the metal available in the temples on the Acropolis. Seven statues of Victory were melted down and a total of fourteen talents of gold or eighty four thousand gold staters was produced. With gold valued at twelve times the value of silver, each gold stater (didrachm) was the equivalent of six silver tetradrachms. At the same time, small denomination coinage was produced in the form of copper pieces, some apparently covered with a plating of silver (**114**).

Production of coinage

The process by which metal was turned into coinage involved a number of stages. As well as requiring the basic technology for refining the raw metals to the required standards, the mints also needed specialist equipment and personnel: artists, craftsmen and labourers. The standard ancient methods of refining precious metals were known long before the invention of coinage; afterwards, the main advances in this field were in the controlled debasing of precious metal coins and the development of base metal alloys suitable for coinage.

Most ancient Greek coins were manufactured by the process known as 'striking'. The blank of metal was placed between two dies and the coin was produced when the upper die was struck by the blow of a hammer, leaving the imprints of the two dies on the two sides of the blank. The blanks could be prepared in a number of ways, though usually they were cast in moulds. With precious metal coins priority was given to the weight of the blank, which was carefully controlled, and also the fineness of the metal, which was usually as fine as refining techniques could achieve. One very interesting and unusual gold coin (**177**), issued under the Egyptian pharaoh Nectanebo II (359-343 BC), actually declared its fineness by way of its design, with two hieroglyphic characters, collar with beads, and heart and windpipe, which translate as 'good gold'.

Usually the metal, from whatever source, would be refined to the appropriate standard before being prepared into the shape of blanks for striking. But sometimes new coins were produced by the restriking of existing coins. These are called 'overstrikes' when traces of the earlier design, which should have been obliterated, are still visible and they can provide important clues for the chronologies of coinage issues when it is possible to identify the design underneath. A famous example, crucial for the chronology of Athenian coinage in the Hellenistic period, has already been mentioned (*see* chapter 1). Overstriking was an inexpensive method of producing local coinage for areas lacking natural supplies of the appropriate metals. Most of the early silver coinage of Crete (**133**), dating from the fifth and fourth centuries BC, was produced in this way. By converting well known 'trade' coins, such as Aeginetan staters, into Cretan city issues, the Cretans managed to retain the much valued silver on their island, since the Cretan coins did not apparently travel abroad.

The dies used for striking most ancient Greek coins were probably made of hardened bronze. Few, if any, official dies have survived. When a die was no longer needed, because it was too worn, badly damaged, or in some other way had become redundant, it would usually have been destroyed in order to prevent possible fraudulent usage, or deposited for safe-keeping in a temple, as we know happened at Athens in the late fifth century BC. Various attempts have been made to estimate the output of ancient coin dies, either by calculation on the basis of documentary and numismatic evidence or by practical experiment using ancient minting techniques. Estimates have ranged from about six thousand to more than forty five thousand coins for a full die life. The actual output of Greek coin dies would have been immensely variable, depending on factors such as the size of the coins to be struck, the hardness and temperature of the blanks, and the number of coins and quality of strikings required at the time. The longest recorded survival of a die in use is at Dalisandus in Lycaonia (southern Turkey), where a reverse die first used in the period AD 161-9 was brought back into use in the reign of Philip (AD 244-9).

The greatest problem in attempting to assess die output accurately is the shortage of documentary evidence. One of the few issues of Greek coinage for which minting accounts survive is that produced in the 330s by the Amphictions (tribal representatives) who governed Delphi (**182**). Fragments of inscriptions recording the Amphictionic treasurers' accounts allow an estimation of the total output of new coinage struck. This was in the range of 125 to 175 talents of silver. By dividing this total by the number of dies estimated to have been used (it is believed that examples struck from virtually all the original dies have by now been recorded) the total die output has been calculated at somewhere within the range of twenty three thousand to forty seven thousand coins for each obverse die, and half these figures for each reverse die.

Occasions of issue

As coinage was the medium with which the Greek cities and kingdoms usually transacted their financial business, such as the payment of expenses and salaries and the collection of revenues, it is only natural that coinage output should have been related to fiscal needs. Not only would overall output have been regulated in this way, but also production of different denominations, since the size and value of a coin would have affected its usefulness for any specific function.

Military expenses were particularly important in ancient finances, mainly because wars were so frequent. Numerous examples of fund raising for the manning and equipping of armies and fleets, and for other military and related expenses such as the payment of tribute, are listed in Book 2 of the *Oeconomica*. The amount of money needed for military expenses would obviously fluctuate according to the numbers of fighting men mobilised at any given time, so that periods of warfare would naturally require heavy expenditure, whereas in peaceful times armies would be disbanded and much less money would be needed. Also, many states in the Greek world used the services of mercenaries, whose loyalty could only be bought by silver and gold, so it is not surprising that the need to pay mercenaries has often been seen as the explanation for coinage issues. In the late fifth and early fourth centuries BC the silver coins produced at Tarsus in Cilicia at first depict on their reverses Persian soldiers and later Greek hoplites (**171**). It has been argued that these designs show the purpose of this money, which was intended primarily for military pay, and the change of reverse type reflects a difference in the composition of the local satrap's army, which from the beginning of the fourth century (following the end of the Peloponnesian War) included large numbers of Greek mercenaries. In the *Oeconomica* (2, 2, 24) the story is told of Didales (assumed to be the Persian general Datames) duping his mercenaries by pretending to have plenty of silver, but getting out of paying them their dues for the moment with the excuse that he first had to take the silver to the mint at Amisus.

There are a number of other coinage issues with obvious military connections, such as those produced by the Carthaginian invaders in Sicily from about 410-290 BC, some of which are marked with the Punic word for 'the camp' (**88**), and the coinage of Philip II of Macedon which, according to literary sources, was used for paying mercenaries and buying allies. There was also the immense coinage of Alexander the Great, produced at numerous mints during his conquest of the Persian Empire. The military emergency which forced Athens to resort to production of gold coinage in 407/6 BC has already been mentioned. Another occasion which caused an unusual striking of coinage (**179**) was the siege of Olynthus by the Athenian general Timotheus in 363-359 BC (*see* chapter 6). Also recorded in the *Oeconomica* (2, 2 16) is the story of an emergency issue from the city of Clazomenae in Asia Minor. It is alleged that the people of Clazomenae were asked to exchange their silver for a new issue of iron coinage in order to pay a debt of twenty talents owed to Clazomenae's mercenary army. The citizens later received interest when they returned their iron coinage for silver.

As well as military, there were also other State expenses which might have prompted the production of coinage issues. Normal administrative costs, such as the payment of officials and the maintenance of public works (harbours, highways and buildings) would usually have been covered by regular income raised in taxation, but a sufficient amount of coinage had to be kept in circulation to support this system, taking into consideration the loss of coins through hoarding and trade. Also, occasional heavy expenditure on public works was necessary. The Amphictionic coinage of Delphi in the 330s (**182**) was issued mainly to pay for the rebuilding of the Temple of Apollo; and in the second half of the fifth century BC massive amounts of silver were turned into Athenian coinage to pay for the great building programme on the Acropolis. No doubt other coinage issues from the Greek world were directly connected with public works. Festivals in ancient Greece could also be very expensive: the people of Antissa in Lesbos are reported to have had problems meeting the costs of celebrating the festival of Dionysus (*Oeconomica* 2, 2, 6). Great festivals might well have provided occasions for coinage issues; for example, the outstanding coinage of Elis (**131-2**) is presumed to have been connected with the Olympic Games, over which the Eleans presided.

Another important motive for coinage production was profit. Metal struck into coin had to be given more value than its worth in bullion in order to pay for the costs of production, and the State could maximise the profitability by making it obligatory for certain official payments to be met in standard coins. This system of forcing an 'official' coinage on the population could easily be abused by unscrupulous rulers and several examples of exploitation are given in Book 2 of the *Oeconomica*. It is alleged that at Athens the tyrant Hippias (527-510 BC) once called in the existing silver coinage, presumably claiming that it needed to be recoined, but he then reissued the same silver, gaining any premiums charged on reissue. This anecdote has been linked with the introduction of the famous owl tetradrachms. Dionysius I, tyrant of Syracuse (405-367 BC), was supposedly even more outrageous in his manipulation of the currency and State finances. On one occasion he is said to have minted a coinage of tin and compelled his citizens to accept it as silver. He also indulged in the fraudulent restriking of silver: 'On another occasion he had borrowed money from the citizens, promising to repay it. On their demanding its return, he bade each bring him, under pain of death, whatever silver he possessed. This silver when brought he coined into drachmae each bearing the face value of two: with these he repaid the (previous) debt and also what had just been brought in.' (*Oeconomica* 2, 2, 20).

Coinage regulation and international cooperation

Large issues of coinage must have been highly profitable as long as the value of coin in trade could be regulated to the advantage of the coin producer. The Aeginetans were famous traders and although they possessed no silver resources of their own they still managed to produce plenty of coinage for their business purposes. The Athenians also required a massive output of silver currency for their activities, commercial and otherwise, and they clearly profited from the exportation of their money. The famous fifth century Coinage Decree is believed to have been an attempt on the part of Athens to monopolise the production of coinage within its 'Empire'. As a result this inscription has received much attention from historians (*see* chapter 5). The decree was set up in all cities of the Delian Confederacy and fragments have been found at Siphnos, Cos, Aphytis in Macedonia and elsewhere. It was in fact a decree of weights and measures which included coinage; there was to be uniformity throughout the Confederacy and silver coinage was not to be struck by member states. It is normally affirmed that this was a law of the mid-fifth century BC, at the height of Athens' power. Recent research has shown, however, that if it was, hardly any of the states that were coining before the promulgation of the law ceased to coin immediately afterwards. A joking reference to the decree in the *Birds* of Aristophanes, produced in spring 414 BC, suggests that the law was at that date still a matter of topical relevance, so the weight of evidence would seem to point to this being a law of the time of the Peloponnesian War. It is usually believed that this was an imperialist act on the part of

Athens, since it involved the imposition of Athenian weights, measures and coinage on the Confederacy. However, if the decree belongs to the 420s it probably had more to do with profit and administrative convenience, since Athens could hardly have wanted to risk antagonizing her allies with a deliberately imperialist act at a time when the war was at its height. On the other hand, the Athenian war machine might work more efficiently if there was some guarantee that quantities of money and goods were fully understood by all concerned.

It is by no means impossible that Athens' opponents in the Peloponnesian League had a little earlier already come to an agreement on coinage production which had a similar effect. It is an extraordinary fact that the coinage of Corinth, which had flourished in the late archaic period and in the mid-fifth century BC, comes to a sudden halt at the beginning of the Peloponnesian War (*see* chapter 5), at the very time when her military expenses must have been on the increase. Corinth was a major participant in the Peloponnesian alliance, and this phenomenon requires some explanation. Corinth may have lost some revenues from taxes imposed during peaceful times on trade passing across the Isthmus. However, at the beginning of the Peloponnesian War the coinage of Sicyon, which had earlier been of only minor importance, springs into prominence and she becomes one of the major coin-producing states of the Peloponnese. The staters of Sicyon, like those of Elis, were on the Aeginetic standard, and as far as the production of coinage in the area is concerned it would seem that the Corinthian standard gave way for the duration of the war to the Aeginetic standard. No fragment of a law enacting such a change of this nature in the economy of the Peloponnese has survived, but from the chronology of the coins themselves it seems likely that this was a conscious decision. There also exists an inscription, usually dated to about 427 BC, listing donations to the Peloponnesian cause, and these are tariffed in gold darics and silver on the Aeginetic standard, suggesting that by this date these were the official forms of currency for the League states.

Alliance coinages more obviously so marked are also to be found. The most famous is the group of coinages which share a design, a figure of the infant Heracles strangling snakes, and on which the ethnic is replaced with the letters Σ YN, clearly indicating the word συμμαχια(alliance). In addition, the staters were all struck to a weight that was not otherwise used. The member states, identifiable by the city types on the other side of the coin, were Rhodes, Cnidus, Iasos, Samos, Ephesus (**147**), Cyzicus and Byzantium. No other traces of such an alliance have survived, but the coins may be dated to the early fourth century BC (*see* chapter 5).

A prominent alliance coinage is that of the Boeotian Confederacy. In the archaic period it was customary for the member cities to mark each issue with their initials, but all used the Boeotian shield as the obverse device and all accepted the Aeginetic weight standard. This continued in the fifth century BC, but individual reverse designs were introduced and Thebes became prominent as the main mint. In the fourth century the federal nature of the currency is emphasised by issues in the name of all the Boeotians, and others without ethnic, signed with the personal names of those responsible for the minting. Such a uniform alliance coinage had many beneficial aspects, with the acceptance of the whole coinage in all cities of the Confederacy.

Monetary alliances were also formed by the two states of Phocaea and Mytilene, whose agreement to share production of fractional electrum coins is preserved on a decree (*see* chapters 5 and 7); and by the cities of Byzantium and Calchedon who collaborated more than once in producing similar coinage issues (*see* chapters 5 and 8). A late fifth to fourth century BC alliance is also clearly visible in the coinages of Campania in Italy, where the coins reveal close cooperation in design and minting procedures and coins of different cities could share a common die, probably because the cities shared the same mint facilities.

Authority, responsibility and coin designs

In the ancient Greek world coins were issued not only by free cities, either individually or in federations or alliances, but also sometimes by cities or other political units that owed allegiance to a greater power. For the latter, formal permission from the higher authority was sometimes required before an issue could be produced. An example of the granting of coining rights exists in the First Book of the Maccabees (1, 15), where the Seleucid King Antiochus VII (138-129 BC) grants the privilege of coining to Simon Maccabaeus, high priest of the Jews: 'I give you leave also to coin money for your country with your own stamp.' Whether such a notion of sovereignty over coinage existed much earlier is by no means clear. Evidence for an objection to local coinage on the part of the Persian kings has been seen in a passage in Herodotus (4, 166) which refers to the removal of the satrap of Egypt, Aryandes, by Darius I: 'Darius had coined money out of gold refined to an extreme purity, and Aryandes, then ruling Egypt, made a like silver coinage ... But when Darius heard that Aryandes was so doing he put him to death, not on this plea but as a rebel.' However, the numerous coinages issued by Greek cities and others under Persian domination suggests that no general ban existed under the Achaemenids.

Aristotle (*Politics* 1, 9, 1257a) observed that the design impressed onto a coin was its essential feature. This mark guaranteed its value by identifying the issuing authority, and on Greek coinage whenever the authority can be identified, for example by an accompanying inscription, it seems invariably to have been the State or an individual acting for the State. This authority was vital to the coin and it is not surprising that most ancient Greek coins were known by the names of their issuing cities, e.g. *Kyzikenoi* ('coins of Cyzicus'), or of the rulers whose authority lay behind them: 'Darics', 'Philips', 'Alexanders'. However, some coins were known by the designs which identified them, for example, the 'owls' of Athens, the 'tortoises' of Aegina, and the 'colts' of Corinth (named after the Pegasus type). These cities each issued large coinages with unchanging designs so that 'owl' was simply a shorthand or nickname for 'coin of Athens'; there was still an implicit recognition of the authority of the coin issuer, since the owl acted as a kind of 'coat of arms' of the city. In chapters 2 and 3 we have already seen numerous examples of coin designs which can be interpreted as the official badges or coats of arms of Greek city-states. This was obviously an appropriate design for an official state-produced coin to carry. It was easy to recognize and was therefore convenient for administrative purposes; but also, it could be used to promote or advertise the state.

The two major elements of a coin design are the picture, or 'type', and the inscription, or 'legend'. The derivation of the word 'type' from the Greek τύπος has already been mentioned (in chapter 2); the word 'legend' derives from the Latin verb *legere*, meaning 'to read'. When the legend gives the name of the issuing people it is often referred to as an 'ethnic', from the Greek word ʾέθνος, meaning a nation or people. The 'owls' of Athens (**108**) provide a clear example of coin-issuer identification through their designs. The obverse has a head of Athena, patron goddess of the city, as its type; the reverse depicts the owl, familiar attribute of Athena and therefore symbolic of the goddess, together with the legend AΘE, which is an abbreviated form of the city's name.

Few Greek coins of the sixth and fifth centuries BC are as explicit in identifying themselves as the 'owls' of Athens. The rarity of recognizable ethnics, especially on the earliest issues, has meant that some coinages can still not be identified with certainty. The major coinage of Corinth escaped attribution for a long time because its identifying initial, the archaic letter *koppa*, went unrecognized, and so many examples of the 'colts' were discovered in Sicily that this was once thought to have been their area of origin. Variety in coin designs also presents problems. The lack of inscriptions and the large number of different designs on the early electrum coinage of Asia Minor has always made it difficult to attribute these pieces, and the same applies to the early Athenian *Wappenmünzen*. It has often been proposed that these were private, not State-sponsored, issues, marked with the 'seals' of individuals; though, as we have already mentioned, an individual might have produced coinage and signed it with his own mark on behalf of, and under the authority of, the State. Identification of coinage issues was certainly made easier once city-states, such as Athens, adopted the practice of consistently using a single design, or combination of obverse and reverse designs, to indicate unambiguously the authority behind their coins.

The categories into which Greek coin designs can be divided are many and varied: heads or figures of favoured deities, attributes of deities, especially animals associated with them such as the eagle of Zeus or the owl of Athens, characters from mythology or local legends, local products or other features identifiable to a specific city or country, and designs which provide a pun on the name of the issuer. All these categories of coin types are represented on Greek coinage of the sixth to fourth centuries, and many examples have already been mentioned in chapters 2 and 3. In the early part of this period animal types are particularly common. Many early coin designs have the appearance of being 'heraldic' devices, and this probably helps to explain the frequent appearance of animals, animal parts (particularly heads or foreparts) and other simple types. Heads of deities are rare on the earliest coins, but in the fifth and fourth centuries BC they became increasingly common. The head was obviously a suitable type in the technical sense because it was essentially a round design, and from the fifth century most coins were round in shape. Also, the wide distribution and commonness of Athenian coins displaying the head of Athena may have contributed to the growing popularity of heads on coins. By the fourth century the head, usually of a deity or other mythological figure, had become an established convention for coin designs in many parts of the Greek world, and at this time also the concept of portraiture, which seems to have had its origins in the East, was spreading. After Alexander the Great's conquest of the Persian Empire the Greek world underwent a radical transformation; no longer was it dominated by independent city-states, but instead the leading powers were the kingdoms formed out of Alexander's empire, and on the coinage of these kingdoms portraits of rulers tended to replace the earlier heads of gods or goddesses. These coins, which usually had a seated or standing figure of a deity on the reverse, became the effective prototypes for the coinage of Imperial Rome and, ultimately, modern coins.

It has already been noted that some Greek cities produced coins with unchanging designs. In particular this is a feature of the major trading cities, such as Athens and Corinth, and also the coinage of Greece's great enemy, the Persian Empire. In fact, most Greek cities used only a limited repertoire of types, because the purpose of the type was to identify the coin, and frequently repeated designs or symbols were the easiest to recognize. Changes in political control at a city might occasion changes in coin designs. New coin types which were introduced as a result of political changes can usually be recognized and they can be important historical documents. Other changes may have resulted from internal administrative reforms, not necessarily linked to other factors, such as politics. Some cities, notably Metapontum in Italy and Abdera in Thrace, sometimes combined an unchanging city type on one side of the coin with a regularly changing design on the other side. In the case of Abdera the changing types are clearly linked to the officials who signed the coins. Also, in some areas, such as Lycia in the fifth century and Cilicia in the early fourth century BC, the copying of designs from the many foreign coins which must have reached these parts seems to have contributed to the diversity in local coin types. The influence of the artists employed to produce the coin dies should not be overlooked.

Another important feature of Greek coin designs is the use of subsidiary pictorial elements, usually referred to as symbols, which sometimes appear alongside the major type. These are rare in the earliest coinages, but they occur with increasing frequency from the fifth century BC. They often seem to have acted as control marks, by identifying the official directly responsible for the authorisation of a particular issue of coinage. In this way they would have had the same purpose as a signature, and they sometimes occur alongside names or monograms.

In the fifth and fourth centuries BC the cities of Cyzicus and Phocaea in Asia Minor reversed the usual functions of the type and symbol. They issued electrum coinages with unchanging symbols – a tunny fish at Cyzicus (**121-2**) and a tiny seal at Phocaea (**123**) – representing the city, accompanying continually changing main types. At this time very few electrum coinages were being produced so there was little need to emphasise the origins of these coins; they were familiar to all who used them, and indeed the third city producing electrum, Mytilene (**124**), did not use an identifying badge at all.

These electrum coinages were uninscribed, as also were most of the earlier electrum issues of Asia Minor. One of the few early electrum coins that does carry an inscription, however, has one that is unusually explicit. The electrum stater with a grazing stag design, already mentioned in chapter 2, has a legend which reads: 'I am the badge of Phanes' (**11**). The inscription clearly identifies the issuing authority. An early fifth century silver coin from Macedonia is equally explicit, reading: 'nomisma (coin) of Getas, King of the Edoni' (**53**). The authority behind this coin is positively identified as the ruler, and there are other names on early Greek silver coins that can be identified as kings, notably on coinages from Lycia and Cyprus. However, before the fourth century names of rulers are relatively uncommon on Greek coins. Ethnics appear much more frequently, though often only in abbreviated form. When the ethnic does appear in full it is most frequently in the genitive case, for example, ΣΥΡΑΚΟΣΙΩΝ ('of the Syracusans'), with the subject of the phrase ('coin' or 'badge') understood.

Other inscriptions on Greek coins include names which identify figures represented on the designs, such as local river gods or city founders, names of denominations, though these are exceedingly rare and mostly confined to later Greek coinages and, much more commonly, names that indicate in some way personal responsibility for the issues. The names of individuals and their offices found on Greek coins are of considerable interest both for our knowledge of the workings of the production of coinage, and for the family histories of the individuals concerned. These may sometimes have been wealthy citizens who personally sponsored the coinage as a form of 'liturgy' (public work), and in the Roman period a name followed by the verb ΑΝΕΘΗΚΕ (dedicated or donated) is a common occurrence and leaves no room for doubt that in the cities of the Roman provinces in Asia Minor such a practice for issues of bronze coinage was widespread. However, to generalize from this that the names on earlier precious metal issues might reflect a similar function is unwarranted. On the coins of the classical period, where there is any indication of the function of the name it is the preposition ΕΠΙ ('in the time of ...') that is expressed, with the name of the person in the genitive case. This refers to a particular period of office, first found in the mid-fifth century BC at Abdera, and through marking the person responsible for the issue this is clearly a form of dating. The reason for the inclusion of the name is the need to protect against malpractice in the production of coins. Wherever the name is in the genitive, as is very often the case, without preposition, it may be assumed that the name acts similarly as a date.

The first coinage to be dated according to an era is the issue made by the Samian exiles who, in 494 BC, found refuge at Zancle (**68**) in Sicily. The sequence of letters A to E undoubtedly represent years based upon the date of the Samians' arrival. The Z on an obol of this series in Oxford may be either a further letter in the sequence or, more probably, the initial letter of the town. In Phoenicia regnal dates are found at Sidon in the mid-fourth century BC, using the Aramaic system in which a horizontal stroke represents each 10 and a vertical stroke each 1. Such a system is also to be found at Tyre on the issues of the same date, and with the coming of Alexander the Great Macedonian imperial coinage from the mint of Ake continued this form of dating, and it is found throughout the Hellenistic period on many issues of Phoenicia. The Greek system of numerals used A to Θ as 1 to 9, with the addition of the archaic letter digamma (ϝ) as 6, between E (5) and Z (7). I to Π represented 10 to 80, with the archaic letter koppa (ϙ) as 90. P to Φ represented 100 to 500. On a coin of Mithradates VI of Pontus (**249**) BKΣ is year 222 of the Pontic dynastic era which began in autumn 297 BC, making the piece of 76/75 BC. It is not until the Hellenistic period that such numerals commonly replaced the name of a magistrate as the method of dating.

The magistracies held by those named on the coins are not often given before the Roman period, but under the Roman Empire there is a great variety: ΣΤΡΑΤΗΓΟΣ (general), ΙΕΡΕΥΣ and ΑΡΧΙΕΡΕΥΣ (priest and high priest), ΑΡΧΩΝ (leader of the council), ΓΡΑΜΜΑΤΕΥΣ (secretary to the council), and many others. In late Hellenistic times in Roman Macedonia we find the ΤΑΜΙΑΣ (treasurer) and his Latin equivalent, quaestor. At the same time on the cistophori of the Roman province of Asia struck at Pergamum the monogram of the word Prytanis gives the office which was regularly responsible for the provincial coinage. The Prytaneis as a body were also responsible at this time for an exceptional issue of gold coinage at Smyrna (**261**). A board of seven is found named on bronze coins of Olbia, and it has recently been discovered that a board of examiners (exetastai) appear on a bronze issue at Erythrae in Ionia. In the mid-first century BC the Roman governors (proconsuls) placed their names on cistophori in Latin (**262**), and they are joined by the names in Greek of those actually responsible for the issues.

Coinage and art

The names of artists also sometimes appear on Greek coins. They can usually be distinguished from other names, such as those of magistrates, because they tend to be included within the coin designs in a discrete, and sometimes in an imaginatively discrete, way. For instance, the artist Kimon, working at Syracuse towards the end of the fifth century BC, placed his signature within the design on the reverse of his coins sometimes on the head band peeping out under the abundant hair of the nymph Arethusa and sometimes on one of the small dolphins swimming around her head. Artists' signatures such as these are just like the signatures on paintings. On a coin from Clazomenae in Asia Minor the die-engraver's signature is more explicitly marked ΘΕΟΔΟΤΟΣ ΕΠΟΙΕ ('Theodotos made ...'). Artists' signatures are by no means common; only on the coins of Sicily at the end of the fifth century BC do they appear at all frequently. However, the artistry displayed on coin designs is a significant feature of the coinage produced in most parts of the Greek world. Although coins were made to be functional objects they also bore the recognizable stamp of their issuers and the Greek city-states and other authorities obviously took pride in their coins. There can otherwise by no explanation for the extraordinarily high level of art which developed, and which culminated in the designs on Sicilian coins signed by the artists who engraved their dies in the late fifth century.

The artistic quality of Greek coin designs has always been one of their main attractions. Before the development of more scientific criteria for classifying Greek coinages they tended to be arranged into chronological groupings based almost entirely on stylistic considerations. Coin designs were compared with other examples of Greek art, stylistic similarities were held to indicate contemporary work, and the coins were then grouped together in 'periods' under subjective headings like 'Period of Finest Art', 'Period of the Decline of Art' and even 'Period of Continual Decline in Art'. These outmoded and prejudicial terms are now no longer used. There is still good reason, however, to include coin designs in the study of ancient art history because coins can be dated much more securely than other artefacts, their place of manufacture is usually certain and they have survived in large numbers and from many different areas of the Greek world. This means that they can be used to reveal changing patterns in artistic style between different periods and regions, and when many examples of a single coin issue are gathered together, the study of the hands of individual die-engravers becomes possible.

The technique of die engraving developed from the much older craft of sealstone cutting. Once coinage had been invented it is likely that the same artists would have worked at both gem and die engraving. Not only was the technique similar, but also both involved work in miniature and on usually round or ovoid-shaped areas. The suitability of heads for coin designs has already been mentioned. Other designs were also arranged in ways which made the most effective use of the surface area available, such as the confronting lion and bull foreparts on the generally ovoid 'Croeseids' (**13**) and on round coins the lion-on-prey compositions seen frequently in north Greece (**47**). Animals were often depicted looking backwards over their shoulder because the overall shape produced fits better within a rounded frame than a forward looking animal. Sometimes extra elements were added in the field around the main type in order to improve the overall balance of the composition, and when symbols or inscriptions had to be included they were usually placed in a way which complemented the rest of the design.

One of the greatest of the Syracusan coinage-die engravers, Kimon, has already been mentioned. Others whose names are recorded on the silver tetradrachms and decadrachms of late fifth century Syracuse include Euainetos, Eukleidas and Phrygillos. These and other artists also worked elsewhere in Sicily and south Italy, signing coins at, for instance, Acragas, Camarina, Catana and Terina, cities now all famous for the beauty of their ancient coin designs. Indeed, many have long been recognized as truly great works of art. The head of Arethusa with her hair held in a net on the Syracusan decadrachms signed by Kimon (**81**) is a masterpiece of miniature sculpture, as also is the beautiful Arethusa head on the Syracusan coins signed by Euainetos (**82**). Kimon also produced probably the finest facing head ever to appear on a coin (**84**). The facing helmeted head of Arethusa by Eukleidas (**85**), on a Syracusan tetradrachm like the facing Arethusa by Kimon, is another brilliant design, as also is the dynamic chariot group on the other (obverse) side of this coin. The chariot groups on most of the Syracusan coins of this period have exceptional artistic qualities and so also do the chariots on coins of Catana (some signed by Euainetos) and on the famous unsigned decadrachm of Acragas (**83**). On this particular coin there is no ground line included underneath the chariot, which gives the effect of flight to the composition, hence its identification with the chariot of Helios. On the other side of the coin is one of the finest animal studies depicted on a Greek coin, showing two eagles with their prey, a hare. This composition illustrates the Greeks' ability to observe nature and to record it with great accuracy and feeling.

The ancient Greeks themselves clearly had an awareness of the artistic merits of coins. Designs were copied from city to city and it is significant that it was not just the commonest, and therefore most familiar types, such as the 'owls' of Athens, that were imitated, but also some much rarer, though beautiful, designs. It is not surprising that the designs on the Syracusan coinage should have been copied widely in the West, and indeed there is no shortage of imitations of the chariot scene in Sicily, even on the coins of the Carthaginian invaders of the island, who also imitated the Arethusa head type, showing an understandable preference for the Euainetos version. But more telling is the appearance in Greece (**143**: Larissa in Thessaly) of the facing head of a nymph, clearly copying the head of Arethusa by Kimon, since Sicilian coins only very rarely appeared in the eastern Mediterranean. The design must have been selected for copying for purely aesthetic reasons, and it also spread further east, appearing again on the coins of the Persian satrap Pharnabazus minted at Tarsus in Cilicia in the 370s (**172**), at the same time as the nearby cities of Soli and Mallus (**173**) were producing coins with equally attractive designs clearly copied from the coins of Heraclea in south Italy. But perhaps the most striking example of the copying of Syracusan masterpieces in the east is provided by a coin of the Lycian dynast Zagaba (**86**) which reproduces the facing head on Eukleidas's Syracusan tetradrachm (**85**), but with the artist's name, cut in minute letters across the visor of the helmet, replaced by the mint name, Antiphellus in Lycian script.

CHAPTER 5

The Classical period

The Greeks were profoundly inspired by their victories over the barbarians of both Persia and Carthage in 480 and 479 BC, and the resulting political and commercial ascendancy of the Greek people, and in particular of the Athenians, was complemented by an upsurge in intellectual and artistic activity. The term 'Classical' is often used to describe the period of Greek history from 479 BC to the time of Alexander, during which many of the great achievements of Greek civilisation were recorded. Coinage was by this time playing an important part in social and economic life in many parts of the Mediterranean world, and because coins were made of a durable material, metal, and were often concealed as valuables, they have survived today in large quantities. Also, as coins were official products of the city-states and were issued not just by the large and powerful states but also by many smaller communities outside the mainstream of Greek history, these surviving coins are an important source of evidence for almost every corner of the Classical Greek world, at times providing, because of their susceptibility to closer dating than most other artefacts, a commentary on the political, economic and artistic history of the various communities which produced them.

In 479 BC the vast majority of the coinage in circulation was silver. By the end of the classical period silver was still the dominant metal for Greek coinage, but by the mid-fourth century there was also widespread production of more valuable gold coinage and less valuable bronze coinage. The range of denominations and hence the usefulness of coinage was therefore much extended. Another important feature of this period was the continuing spread of coinage into regions that had previously not produced it, notably east into the Levant and south into Egypt. Because of the extensive geographical range of Greek coinage it is again

Fig. 7   *Greece in the Classical period*

convenient to look at each region in turn and for this period we can
proceed from west to east, beginning where we left off in chapter 3.

The West: Sicily

The tyrannies which controlled most of the Greek cities of Sicily in 480
BC continued to dominate the island's history until the 460s. Gelon's
fortunes were much enhanced by his victory at the battle of Himera. The
spoils of war, plus an indemnity of two thousand talents (equivalent to
three million tetradrachms) which the defeated Carthaginians had to
pay, enriched Syracuse, so it is not surprising that the period following
480 BC saw a great increase in output of Syracusan coinage. The standard
silver coin of Syracuse, the tetradrachm, had designs on both sides, as
indeed did all the Sicilian coins from this period on. The obverse shows a

chariot crowned by Nike (thought to be an allusion to Gelon's Olympic victory of 488 BC); on the reverse is a head of Arethusa encircled by four dolphins. The most famous representative from this phase of Syracusan coinage is the decadrachm, often, though probably misleadingly, referred to as the 'Demareteion'. (**70**).

Gelon himself died in 478 or 477 BC but his family remained in power, with his brother Hieron ruling Syracuse and another brother, Polyzalos, ruling Gela. In the cities dominated by these men the growing influence of Syracuse can be seen on the coinages, which often adopted the Syracusan denominations and the chariot design. At Gela (**71**)the chariot is coupled with the forepart of a man-faced bull, the local river god and badge of the city. At the inland city of Leontini (**72**), which was controlled by Syracuse and enlarged in 476 BC by the arrival of citizens expelled from Catana and Naxos by Hieron, the reverse design shows a lion's head surrounded by four grains of barley, which is a local translation of the head of Arethusa-with-dolphins composition of Syracuse. At Himera (**73**), which was under the control of Acragas until 470 BC, when the Acragantine tyranny was overthrown by Syracuse, the city's earlier coin designs, featuring a cock, were replaced by new issues with a chariot, again showing the influence of Syracuse, and an interesting reverse depicting the local river goddess at an altar accompanied by a small figure of Silenus bathing in water falling from a spout in the shape of a lion's head.

The tyrannies of Syracuse and Rhegium did not long survive that of Acragas, and by the end of the 460s the Sicilian cities were once more being governed by their own citizens, in some cases, notably Camarina, Catana and Naxos, returning after enforced exile following their removal under the tyrants. Not surprisingly, new coin designs appeared in some cities, although at others the changes in political power left little visible effect on the coinage. At Naxos (**74**) the restored population produced one of the finest of all Greek coins, depicting on the obverse a superb bearded head of Dionysus and on the reverse a squatting Selinus. An equally fine, and so far unique piece, thought by some to be by the same artist, was struck in the name of the people of Aetna (**75**), possibly after their removal from the city of Catana-Aetna when it was reinhabited by its former population. (Earlier, the Catanians had been removed by Hieron and their city renamed Aetna). The Aetna coin depicts a remarkable head of Silenus on the obverse, and on the reverse a composition featuring a seated Zeus with an eagle on a pine tree.

The second half of the fifth century BC was the great period of civic coinage in Sicily, with the many independent cities producing coins with the most attractive and ambitious designs, culminating in the signed tetradrachms and decadrachms which we have already mentioned in chapter 4. The influence of Syracuse continues to be visible throughout this period, with changes in its coin designs being mirrored elsewhere. Thus, after the sedately walking chariot was replaced at Syracuse by a galloping chariot it was not long before similar galloping chariots began appearing at other cities throughout the island.

Another important feature of the Sicilian coinage of this period is the first appearance of a new metal, bronze. The non-Greek people of the interior in both south Italy and Sicily (the Sicels) used bronze for measuring values, and when the Greek cities of Sicily produced the first bronze coins these were made to match the native weight standard, the *litra*, which was divided into twelve *unciae*. Bronze coins extended the range of coinage down into much lower values than could earlier be conveniently transacted. They soon spread to southern Italy and eventually to the rest of the Greek world. The earliest Sicilian bronzes were produced by casting and some have unconventional shapes; one group, from Acragas and dating from about 435 BC, was cast into cone shapes (**77**). A little later the same city issued conventionally shaped, struck bronze coins (**78**). Both these and the 'cones' were marked with pellets to indicate their denominations in unciae; for example, two pellets = two unciae = sixth-litra, three pellets = three unciae = quarter-litra, six pellets = six unciae = half-litra.

Towards the end of the fifth century BC, Sicily's relatively peaceful progress was shattered. First came the invasion from Athens in 415 BC, successfully beaten back by Syracuse; next came the great invasions by Carthage. Phoenicians and, later, Carthaginians, had long been settled in western Sicily in the cities of Motya, Panormus and Solus. The defeat of the earlier Carthaginian invasion of 480 BC had not rebounded on these Punic settlements and when the next invasions began in the last decade of the fifth century they were again used as a base of operations by the Carthaginians. In the first incursion of 410/9 BC the cities of Himera and Selinus were taken by the invaders; the great city of Acragas fell in 406 BC, and within a few years Syracuse was the only Greek city on the island still maintaining its independence.

The progress of the Carthaginian invaders provides fixed dates for the chronologies of some Sicilian coinages. For instance, we know that the long series of fifth century coinage issues from Acragas, which culminated with the magnificent decadrachm (**83**) described in chapter 4, must have ended by 406 BC; also, the clear imitation of Syracusan designs at cities about to fall provides pointers for dating the Syracusan originals. The Carthaginian invaders themselves imitated the coin designs of the Greek cities, particularly Syracuse, though they also issued coins with their own designs (**88**) of a horse and palm tree, together with inscriptions in Punic letters which read 'Carthage' and 'the Camp', identifying the purely military nature of the coinage. The term Siculo-Punic is used to describe these coin issues of the Carthaginians in Sicily.

In the fourth century hostilities between the Greeks of Sicily and the Carthaginians continued. Syracuse was ruled by the tyrant Dionysius I from 405 to 367 BC and in this period the Syracusan coinage is characterised by production of unusually large denomination coins in silver (the decadrachms) and gold, presumably reflecting the need to pay large numbers of mercenaries. The anecdotes concerning Dionysius recorded in the *Oeconomica* certainly suggest that paying mercenaries was one of this ruler's chief concerns. The first gold issues probably date from 406/5 BC when similar pieces were produced by the cities of Acragas and Gela to pay for their defence against the Carthaginians. After 400 BC the gold coins of Syracuse were struck in two denominations, apparently fifty and one hundred litra pieces. As with the earlier tetradrachms the obverse type depicts a head of Arethusa, but on the reverse there is a new design of Heracles fighting the Nemean lion, symbolizing the struggle of the Sicilian Greeks against Carthage (**87**).

In 344 BC Timoleon arrived in Sicily from Corinth, having been invited by Syracuse to assist in the fighting against Carthage. With a series of military successes he managed to liberate a large part of the island, and as a result there was a revival of prosperity in the Greek cities of eastern Sicily. Timoleon's expedition was financed by Corinth and her colonies in north-western Greece, and the coins imported from these cities had a significant impact on the currency of Sicily. Hoards from the island show that Corinthian pegasi became the standard silver coins of the Greeks and local versions were produced at Syracuse (**89**) and Leontini (and also at Locri in southern Italy). At the same time large issues of bronzes were produced at Syracuse with designs – Pegasus (**91**) and heads of Athena (**90**) – that clearly link them with the Corinthian coins. Silver pegasi in fact dominated the currency of Sicily until late in the fourth century when Agathocles, tyrant of Syracuse 317-289 BC, reorganised production of Syracusan coinage, including the revived tetradrachm.

The West: south Italy

The fifth and fourth centuries BC saw significant developments in coinage production in southern Italy. It was also a period of change, with shifts in the balance of power in the separate regions being reflected in output of coinage as old centres declined and new ones took their place.

The first obvious development was the gradual disappearance of the incuse technique, which had given the area its originality in the archaic period. Of the south Italian cities that had produced incuse coinage in the sixth century, Metapontum and Croton continued to employ the technique until about 440 BC, though with an increasingly dumpy fabric, bringing the coins more into line with conventional issues. Caulonia abandoned the incuse technique earlier in the century, producing coins with designs in relief on both sides: on the obverse a standing Apollo and on the reverse a stag (**92**). Similarly, Poseidonia (**93-4**), which had ceased production of incuse coinage at the end of its first phase (*c*.500 BC), also began issuing double relief coins from about 470 BC, with Poseidon on the obverse and a bull on the reverse.

It has been suggested that the appearance of a bull design on the new Poseidonian coinage at this time probably marks the arrival of refugees from the city of Sybaris, which was destroyed again by Croton in 476 BC (following a resettlement after the original destruction of 510 BC). During the fifth century the Sybarites made several attempts to recolonise their ancient city and in between they appeared as refugees in other south Italian cities. The movements of these people can be traced through various coinage issues which link Sybaris or the Sybarites with other cities, notably Poseidonia and Laus. The final refoundation on the original site of Sybaris took place in 446 BC, this time with help from Athens. However, within a few years the Sybarites were expelled yet again and the city was renamed Thurii. The sequence of events is clearly visible on the coinage. At first an Athena head appears on the obverse, coupled with the Sybarite bull with its head turned back and the name of the city ΣYBAPIΣ (**95**); then the bull changes its pose, and soon after the new ethnic ΘOYPIΩN appears (**96**).

Thurii soon became one of the dominant cities in the region. The appearance of its Athena head design on coins of other cities, notably Velia and Heraclea, clearly shows its influence, and evidence of its prosperity can be seen in the long series of heavy two-stater silver coins (**98**) which it issued, beginning late in the fifth century BC. Thurii was also one of the first cities in south Italy to produce bronze coinage (**97**).

The great rival of Thurii on the south coast was the city of Taras, the only colony ever founded by Sparta. Taras produced a few issues of incuse coinage, dating to about 500 BC, but at that time Taras was not a major coin producer. The city's output increased, however, in the course of the fifth century. The standard design on the obverse of the Tarentine silver stater was at first a young dolphin rider, usually identified as Taras, the son of Poseidon, but from about 430 BC this was replaced by a horseman which, in various forms, was to remain the standard obverse type to the end of Tarentine coinage. Meanwhile, in about 400 BC the dolphin rider reappeared, now on the reverse of the stater, and there it remained as the partner of the horseman, again until the end of coinage production at Taras (**99**). The Tarentines did not favour bronze coinage;

instead, for their local small denomination coins they issued a wide range of silver fractions (**100**). Production of the largest of these, the diobol, was shared with the city of Heraclea (**101**) (founded jointly by Taras and Thurii in 433 BC to control the lands between the two rival cities), and this coin circulated widely in south Italy. It had for its designs a head of Athena on the obverse and Heracles with the Nemean lion on the reverse, the same types that were used for the silver staters of Heraclea.

As with Sicily, it can fairly be said that the most impressive feature of the south Italian coinages of this period is their artistic quality. Here too artists signed coins, notably at the cities of Metapontum, Heraclea and Velia. A good example of the artistic excellence shown by the coinage of the region is provided by the city of Terina, on the west coast of Italy's 'toe'. Originally a colony of Croton, Terina's history is obscure, but it seems the city never attained more than a purely local prominence. However, beginning in the middle of the fifth century BC, Terina produced an attractive and original series of coin issues. The obverse design was invariably a head of the local nymph Terina, while the reverses had Nike in a variety of poses, each slightly different from the others. On the example illustrated (**102**), dating from about 440 BC, she is seated on an amphora, holding a caduceus and a wreath.

The principle denomination of coinage in production throughout southern Italy in this period was the silver stater, weighing about 8 grammes and the evidence of coin hoards suggests that there was considerable movement of coinage between the different cities. But many cities also produced small denomination silver coins and these, together with the bronze pieces which began to appear at some cities before the end of the fifth century BC, remind us of the practical function of coinage in the economies of the city states.

From the later fifth century the Greek cities of southern Italy began to come under increasing pressure from the native Italic tribes of the interior. The first to be affected were the cities of the west coast, notably Cumae and Poseidonia. Cumae, the most northern of the Greek colonies in Italy, had become, by the middle of the fifth century, an important city with a considerable output of coinage. The standard designs on its coins (**103**) were: for the obverse, a head of the local nymph, Kyme, and for the reverse, a mussel shell (apparently the badge of the city, appearing on various denominations). However, in 421 BC the city was captured by the Campanians. A few issues of coinage were subsequently produced in the name of the city, but showing increasing native influence; then production petered out around the end of the century.

When Cumae fell to the Campanians the nearby city of Neapolis took over as the leading Greek city of the area. The rise to prominence of Neapolis is as clearly visible on the coinage as the decline of Cumae. The coinage of Neapolis (**104**) evolved gradually, absorbing influences from Cumae, from Syracuse, from the native Campanians and also from Thurii until, in the middle of the fourth century, it adopted the designs that were to remain standard at the city for the rest of its history. The obverse of its silver stater depicted a head of the siren Parthenope, the reverse featured the river god Achelous, father of the sirens, as a man-faced bull, crowned by a flying Nike. A number of other Campanian cities also struck issues of coinage copying these and earlier Neapolitan coin types, but in the course of the fourth century Neapolis emerged as the sole mint of the region.

Further down the west coast the principal mint was Velia, whose coinage continued apparently uninterrupted through the fifth and into the fourth century BC, by which time output was significantly increased. Velia was one of the cities which adopted the Athena head, copied from Thurii, for its obverse design, while the reverse retained the lion, surviving from the city's earliest issues, either alone or attacking a stag. The coin designs of Velia were often beautifully executed; the example illustrated (**105**) bears the signature of the artist Philistion on the helmet of Athena.

The growing threat of the Italic tribes was also felt on the eastern side of south Italy, and in the extreme south disruption was also caused by the aggression of Dionysius I of Syracuse. A particularly noticeable feature of the fourth century BC coinage of the region as a whole is the presence of large denomination pieces, including occasional gold issues. The purpose of these was doubtless to pay the mercenaries which were employed to defend the cities. From the middle of the fourth century a series of 'condottieri', together with their mercenary forces, were invited from Greece to help defend the Greek colonies in Italy (*see* chapter 7).

Before leaving the western Mediterranean mention should be made of the coins issued in this region outside Italy and Sicily. The production of early fifth century 'Auriol' coins in southern France has already been mentioned (*see* chapter 3), and it seems that similar small pieces were also produced in Spain, and in the fourth century the Greek colony of Emporium in north-east Spain began signing coins with the city's initial letters, EM (**106**). Meanwhile the colony of Massalia (Marseilles) was growing in importance and, at the same time, issuing increasing quantities of coinage, at first mostly small denomination pieces, following the 'Auriol' tradition, then, from about 350 BC, drachms weighing about 3.7 grammes. These coins (**107**), which were decorated with a head of Artemis on the obverse and a walking lion on the reverse, became the staple currency over a wide area in southern France and northern Italy, and were extensively copied by Celtic tribes.

Athens and her allies in the Aegean

Following the defeat of the Persians in 479 BC Athens emerged as the dominant power in the Aegean. The Delian League was formed, with Athens its elected leader, to defend the Aegean against further Persian attacks and to liberate Greek cities still under Persian domination. The league members, which included most Greek cities of the northern and eastern Aegean coastlands, as well as the islands, contributed either ships or money to a treasury which was kept at Delos. However, Athens soon began to transform this confederacy of allies into an empire. Cities which fell out with Athens, such as Naxos in 469 and Thasos in 465-3 BC, were invariably forced back into the league with reduced status, as subject tributary allies deprived of their autonomy. Other states were forced against their will to join the league. Then, in 454 BC the treasury was transferred to Athens and although, following a negotiated peace with Persia, there was now no obvious threat from Persia, the 'contributions' of the allies continued to be collected by Athens, by force if necessary.

Athens thus became the capital city of an empire. With a huge fleet to maintain, territories to defend and adminster, and an expensive building programme for the Acropolis to finance, the city obviously had need of much coinage. It is not surprising then that the 'owls' of Athens continued to be the classical Greek world's most familiar coins. The tried and trusted designs of Athena head and owl were retained for all denominations (**108-13**), with only minor variations to distinguish different values. The most obvious change from the earlier owls of the period before the Persian Wars was the inclusion of a row of laurel leaves on Athena's helmet on the obverse (which is why the term 'wreathed' is used to describe them), and the addition of a crescent moon next to the sprig of olive on the reverse of the tetradrachms and drachmae.

All issues were struck only in silver at first and the tetradrachm was, as before, the principal denomination. The various issues have been arranged into chronological sequence by a meticulous study of stylistic development and the evidence of coin hoards. A recently discovered hoard from the Lycian region of southern Turkey contained one hundred and sixty one 'wreathed' tetradrachms of the 470s and 460s BC, together with fourteen examples of an issue of decadrachms (which have given it the name 'Decadrachm hoard'), the only such issue ever known to have been produced by Athens. Before the discovery of this hoard it was thought, on the basis of the relative scarcity of Athenian coinage of this period, that output at the Athenian mint must have been much lower in the 470s and 460s than at other times. Now it seems this view must be reconsidered; though output did nevertheless increase after the middle of the century when the League treasury money was being used first to finance the Acropolis works and then Athens' war effort following the outbreak of the Peloponnesian War in 431 BC. In that year we are told by Thucydides (II, 13, 3) that Athens still held a reserve of sixty thousand talents, but by 407/6 the city's supplies of silver were apparently all but exhausted. As we have already seen (in chapter 4) Athens had to resort to an emergency issue of gold coinage (**113**) and production of silver-plated copper coins (**114**).

The famous coinage decree of Athens has already been mentioned (*see* chapter 4). If effective it should have resulted in the cessation of local coinage production throughout the Athenian Empire. Unfortunately, the decree cannot be dated with certainty; two alternative dates, the early 440s and 420s BC both have their devotees. It is possible that detailed studies of the coinages of all the mint cities which ought to have been affected by the decree might in time provide a secure date. Though it is difficult to prove a necessary link between the imposition of a coinage decree and a cessation of local coinage when coinage production could at any time be curtailed for many other reasons, if a consistent pattern of independently dated coinage 'gaps' were to emerge this would be significant and the absence of such 'gaps' in the 440s, according to hoards and other evidence, seems already to be undermining the early date.

The recent 'Decadrachm hoard' has provided important evidence for dating the coinages of Athens' allies in the north Aegean. This hoard was buried around 462 BC, some years before the Athenian coinage decree, whatever its date, but because it gives a clear and consistent picture of the stage of development reached by the coinages of various mints at this point it can also be used to date the issues produced subsequently. The impression given is that at the mints of Athens' allies no break in coinage can be seen to fit in with a decree dating from the early 440s. Notably, the major mints of Abdera, Acanthus and Mende all seem to have continued striking coins well after this date. For Mende there is also the evidence of a coin overstruck on a piece from Gela in Sicily that can be dated to the period 450–440 BC.

The most significant developments in north Aegean coinage in the middle of the century were the cessation of the tribal issues that were so characteristic of the earlier period, and also the end of production of the octadrachm and other very large silver pieces. The Bisalti were the major producers of these coins after about 480 BC and then, from the late 460s, Alexander I of Macedon (**116**). Alexander was said at one time to be mining a talent of silver each day from the Lake Prasias mines. However, it seems that these particular north Aegean mines may soon afterwards have been worked out: from the middle of the century no coins larger than the tetradrachm were produced in the area, then later in the century most of the north Aegean mints ceased production altogether. This may have been because of a decree; or perhaps economic pressure from Athenian currency; or maybe the exhaustion of local mineral sources.

The coinages of the north Aegean show some interesting stylistic and typological developments in the fifth century BC. In the 460s a fashion began for placing inscriptions on the reverse of coins within a thin frame surrounding the four sides of a central square. Examples can be seen on the last of the tribal coinages, for instance those of Getas, King of the Edoni, and the Bisalti, on the coins of Alexander of Macedon, and also on the mid-century issues of various cities including Acanthus and Mende (**117**). In their choice of designs the mints tended in general to continue with the same themes that they had used earlier. A notable newcomer was Aenus (**118**) in eastern Thrace, which began minting in the 450s. The standard designs used on this city's coinage in the fifth century were a head of Hermes, the god of herds, on the obverse, and a goat on the reverse.

The cities of the eastern Aegean coastlands and islands were, like those of the north, all members of the Delian League in the fifth century. Again, their coinages should have been affected significantly by the economic dominance of Athens and certainly by any effective coinage decree. However, the coinage of this region is characterised by its diversity and it is difficult to obtain a clear picture of coinage output. Attempts have been made to arrange the chronologies of the various coinages into sequences that would allow a break in the third quarter of the century, to correspond with the imposition of a decree in the early 440s, but there are plenty of examples that do not conform. Samos (**119-20**), a leading member of the League, apparently produced regular issues of its silver coinage throughout the period from about 479 until the 430s BC. In Lycia (**155, 157**), which was incorporated into the League in the 460s, coinage continued right through the second half of the century. It has also recently been argued that Cnidus on the Carian coast issued throughout this period, though a break in output to fit a decree in the 440s has also been claimed. Elsewhere, many mints seem to have ceased production by the middle of the century, before the decree could possibly have been issued. Once again, the evidence of the new Decadrachm hoard is of use. For instance, the issues of silver stater-size coins of the cities of Rhodes, which are abundant in this hoard, can be shown to end around 460 BC, though it seems that silver fractions were issued for a short time after. These later issues also contained some extremely rare small electrum coins.

In the first half of the fifth century many of the cities of the eastern Aegean produced only small denomination silver coins. It seems that for larger denominations in silver they used 'foreign' coins. The evidence of hoards suggests wide circulation of north Aegean coinage and, in some parts, Persian sigloi, and most of all Athenian tetradrachms would have been used. Athens' political domination and the overwhelming abundance of her 'owls' no doubt caused a natural retreat of other rival silver coins. Small denominations would still have been needed for local internal use and city-states with major commercial interests, such as Chios and Samos, or access to plentiful silver sources might still have been able to compete, but it seems that in general locally produced currency in much of the Aegean was already being driven out with or without a coinage decree. We can see clear examples of this nearer to Athens, in Euboea and in the Cycladic islands. Both these areas were prolific coin producers before 479 BC but issued very little after this date.

An exceptional and interesting group of mints in this period is that formed by the electrum issuers of Asia Minor: Cyzicus, Mytilene and Phocaea. The point will be made in chapter 6 that these were obviously not meant to have the same function as the usual city issues. Cyzicus issued electrum staters (**121**) and fractions (**122**). The evidence of finds suggests that this coinage had a major role in international trade between Greece and the Black Sea; they were familiar coins in Athens, being mentioned frequently on inscriptions from the city. The electrum of Mytilene (**124**) and Phocaea (**123**) was issued almost entirely in sixth-stater pieces and, as we have seen, was for a time produced by a joint agreement between the cities. These coins circulated widely in western Asia Minor.

The Cyzicene staters contained designs only on their obverses, but these are immensely interesting and varied, drawing on influences from many other coinages. However, the characteristic tunny fish symbol was always retained as the identifying badge of the city's coinage. Mytilene, on the other hand, is notable for being the one electrum mint to employ designs on both faces of the coins, and for a time in the fifth century it adopted the unusual technique of having the reverse design in intaglio (**124**). The practice was similar to that seen on the earliest issues of the south Italian mints, except that at Mytilene a different type was used on each side of the coin.

Greece in the fifth century

On the Greek side of the Aegean in the period after 479 BC Athens was not the only major power. Areas such as the Peloponnese and western Greece were, for a time at least, largely unaffected by the growth of Athenian imperialism. But in other parts interference from Athens was a regular occurrence and the growing threat posed to the independence of the Greek city-states inevitably led to war with her greatest rival Sparta.

The Peloponnesian War, as it is usually referred to, lasted from 431 to 404 BC. In the course of this war Athens was deserted by her 'allies' and by the time the war ended the defeated city no longer had an empire.

The coinages of Greece must be seen against the background of these political developments. For an example we can look at Aegina, whose fifth century coinage has been put into chronological sequence largely from the evidence of coin hoards. Aegina was one of the most prolific producers of coinage in the archaic period. After 479 BC the island continued to issue its famous 'turtles', though output seems to have been less than before, perhaps reflecting Aegina's decline as Athens gained commercial domination of the Aegean. These later turtles can be distinguished from earlier varieties by the presence of a T-shaped pattern of pellets on the turtle's shell (**33, 34**). In 457 BC Aegina was invaded by Athens and forced to become one of the 'allies'. This event may have caused the next change in the Aeginetan coinage, which was the replacement of the turtle on the obverse with a tortoise (**125**). Interestingly, the reverse retained the simple 'skew' pattern, which had been in use since the archaic period. This phase of Aeginetan coinage would have lasted no later than 431 BC when the island was once more invaded by Athens. On this occasion the entire population was expelled and replaced by Athenian settlers, and no more Aeginetan coinage was subsequently produced until the native inhabitants were restored after the defeat of Athens in 404 BC.

A similar end came to the fifth century coinage of Melos (**126**), in the Cyclades. In 416 the island was invaded by Athens and the entire population was either killed or enslaved. A single hoard found on Melos in 1907 has provided all the known examples of the coinage produced by the island, apparently just before its fall. Most pieces have the traditional badge of Melos, the apple, on the obverse, while the reverses depict a wide variety of different types.

In central Greece again the influence of Athens is evident. The Phocians, at first allies of Athens, produced their small denomination silver pieces, mostly hemidrachms and obols, for most of the century, though output seems to have been reduced following their withdrawal from the Athenian confederacy in 447 BC. Boeotia produced little coinage in the period immediately following 479 BC, but after Athens invaded the area in 456 there seems to have been a revival of city coinages. These, however, came to an end when, after the Athenian withdrawal of 446, the city of Thebes regained its dominance of the area. For the rest of the century Thebes was the only minting city in Boeotia. The coinage produced by Thebes (**127**) at this time was particularly fine in style and interesting in design. The Boeotian shield remained, as usual, on the obverse, but for the reverses there are many different designs.

Most of these feature Heracles and they are surely meant to symbolise the revival of Theban power.

For most of the fifth century the Arcadian League produced a federal coinage, confined, like many other Peloponnesian coinages of the period, to small denominations, triobols and obols, on the Aeginetan weight standard. These coins were likely to have been produced mainly for military payments, since we know that the daily pay for an infantryman in the Peloponnese was three Aeginetan obols (*Thucydides* V, 47). The League coinage was minted at a number of separate cities; the usual designs for the principal denomination, the triobol (**128**), were a figure of Zeus on the obverse and a head of Artemis on the reverse. There were few significant coinages elsewhere in the Peloponnese in the fifth century but in the 420s the city of Sicyon (**129**) began its issues of staters (previously it had produced only smaller denominations) and these coins soon became the most important currency of the region, and indeed circulated widely in other parts of the Greek mainland. The designs on the staters of Sicyon consisted of a chimaera on the obverse and a dove on the reverse. There was also the coinage of the city of Elis, which presided over the Olympic Games. The Elean coinage (**131-2**) has very fine artistic style and it included a higher proportion of large denomination coins (staters) than was usual in the Peloponnese. Its types were dominated by symbols of Olympian Zeus, the eagle and the thunderbolt. Depictions of Zeus also appear and, from the late fifth century, a head of Hera, which is the usual obverse type on a series of coins that are thought to have been issued from a second mint. The coinage of Elis is assumed to be connected with the Olympic Games.

The chief military rival of Athens, Sparta, did not issue coinage, but Athens' principal commercial rival, the city of Corinth, did. The so-called 'Pegasi' were already a familiar, plentiful coinage in the archaic period and production of these coins continued after 479 BC. The designs remained the same, though stylistic changes reflecting broader artistic developments can clearly be seen, notably in the head of Athena which changes from 'archaic' to 'classical' (**134**). Output continued to be high until around the middle of the century; then the issues became intermittent and output dropped until, apparently soon after the outbreak of the Peloponnesian War, the mint of Corinth ceased production altogether. This coincides with the increase in production of coinage at Sicyon mentioned above, and it has been suggested (*see* chapter 4) that this may have been as a result of an agreement between the Peloponnesian states. Meanwhile, Pegasi were also issued by some of Corinth's colonies, notably Leucas (**135**) in western Greece, whose issues continued in the later fifth century after those of Corinth ceased.

Greece and the Aegean in the fourth century

The return to normality following the defeat of Athens led to a revival of coinage at several mints. Aegina resumed its coinage along similar lines to its earlier issues. In Euboea a federal coinage had begun in the last years of the war. This continued in the fourth century and civic issues on the island were also revived. Corinth (**136**) began minting Pegasi again. Output was now greater than ever before; the coins of Corinth and her colonies circulated widely in western Greece and also, as we have seen, in Sicily and south Italy, where the fourth century issues of Pegasi became a staple currency. For both the tortoises of Aegina and the Pegasi the main difference in appearance, when compared with the fifth century issues, is the inclusion within their designs of changing symbols and letters, which were added to identify the persons responsible for each issue.

When Athens resumed production of coinage some years after the city's defeat in 404 BC the base emergency money from the last years of the war was demonetised and new, good silver was produced. The new coins (**137**) copied their fifth century predecessors, though they can be distinguished stylistically. The clearest difference is in the eye of Athena, which in fourth century issues is always seen in profile, as opposed to the earlier frontal appearance. Though fourth century Athenian coinage did not dominate the international trade in silver coin so much as the more abundant fifth century owls, nevertheless the later owls still travelled far, especially to the East, and were, like their predecessors, widely imitated. In the fourth century Athens again, as earlier, issued a wide range of small denomination coins in silver. Not until late in the century did the city begin to replace the smaller silver fractions with regular issues of official bronze coins.

At first, the only major mints in the Peloponnese were at Elis and Sicyon, continuing their fifth century issues. Then, in the 360s there was a widespread revival of both civic and federal issues. It is believed that this may have been connected with the removal of Spartan domination from the area following Sparta's defeat by the Boeotian League at the battle of Leuctra in 371 BC. In many parts of the Peloponnese now, not only were the customary small denomination pieces, triobols and obols, produced, but also larger drachms and didrachm-staters. For these new issues the best die cutters were recruited and the coins they produced stand out as amongst the most beautiful ever struck in Greece. At each mint the usual designs were a profile head of a god or goddess on the obverse and, often, a figure of a deity on the reverse. The shared use of this convention and the consistently fine artistic style gives the various issues of didrachms an overall appearance of conformity. The Arcadian League (**138**) didrachms depict a superb head of Zeus and a seated figure of Heracles; the Messenians used a head of Demeter, based on the heads cut by the artist Euainetos at Syracuse, and a standing Zeus. Argos (**139**) produced a more extensive series of didrachms than most of the other mints (whose issues of didrachms were mostly very short-lived); its types were a head of Hera on the obverse and two dolphins on the reverse. The city of Elis also shared in this increased coining activity. The Eleans lost control of Olympia for the festival of 364 BC, following its seizure by the Arcadians the previous year (this may in fact have been the occasion for the issue of Arcadian League didrachms just mentioned). However, they were back in control by 360 BC and the resumption of festival coinage by Elis is marked by issues with longer legends than usual and with a head of Olympia.

After the victory over Sparta in 371 BC Thebes was not only the leader of the Boeotian League but also, for a few decades, the most powerful city-state in Greece. During its period of supremacy Thebes (**140**) produced issues of staters with the usual Boeotian shield design on the obverse and on the reverse an amphora, accompanied by an abbreviated name again, it can be assumed, identifying the authority responsible for each issue. These coins were minted in large quantities and circulated widely in many parts of Greece, effectively taking over the position earlier occupied by the Sicyonian staters. Elsewhere in central Greece another important fourth century mint was that of the city of Larissa (**143**) in Thessaly, which produced a major series of drachms and didrachms with a facing head of a nymph, clearly copying the Syracusan type by the artist Kimon, on the obverse, and a horse design, obviously appropriate for Thessaly, on the reverse. Equally attractive was the coinage of the Locrians of Opus (**144**). Their issues of staters and smaller denominations used another Syracusan prototype for the obverse design, the Arethusa head by Euainetos, and for the reverse they depicted a figure of the local hero Ajax, of Trojan War fame.

In 356 BC the Phocians took control of Delphi, and during the Sacred War (356-346 BC) which resulted they issued a large series of hemidrachms (**141**) with designs of a frontal bull's head on the obverse and head of Apollo on the reverse. The main purpose of the coinage was the payment of mercenaries fighting for Phocis, and the temple treasures were plundered to help finance these issues. Bronze coins were also produced and these include the names of two Phocian generals, Onymarchus (**142**) and Phalaecus.

In the north Aegean the coinage of the fourth century reveals a number of significant developments, some of which can be related to the changing circumstances occasioned by the Peloponnesian War. A number of cities had rebelled against Athenian domination in the later fifth century: Acanthus, Amphipolis and Mende in 424 BC, Abdera in 411 BC, and as part of a general reaction against Athenian influence when new coinages were inaugurated by the cities of the region they usually adopted a weight system different from that of Athens.

The most important coinage in Macedonia from the later fifth century was that of the Chalcidian League, which was established in 432 BC. From its capital at Olynthus the League issued a major series of tetradrachms (**181**), together with smaller denomination silver pieces. The standard designs employed were a laureate head of Apollo for the obverse and a lyre for the reverse (except for the smallest fractions). Its tetradrachms weighed 14.25 grammes, noticeably less than those of Athens. This new weight system, which is often referred to as the 'Phoenician', was soon adopted by other cities in the region, notably Acanthus, Amphipolis and Mende, presumably because of the commercial importance of the coins of the Chalcidian League. In the fourth century the League also produced occasional issues of gold staters. Other points to note on the fourth century issues of these Macedonian cities are the inclusion of names of officials, which became a regular occurrence on the tetradrachms and also, as so often with the coinage of this period, the high level of artistic style. Particularly attractive are the obverses of the tetradrachms of Amphipolis (**185**), which depict a facing head of Apollo, clearly following the tradition of the facing heads from Syracuse and elsewhere.

In the late fifth and early fourth centuries the Macedonian kingdom was not a major producer of coinage. No longer was there available the abundance of silver which Alexander I had turned into coin. Perdiccas II (about 451–413 BC) issued only small silver tetrobols (four obol pieces); then Archelaus (413–399 BC) and his successors, though they produced staters (weighing about 11 grammes), issued only moderate quantities of silver coin, some of it debased, accompanied by bronzes.

In Thrace the cities freeing themselves from Athenian control at the end of the fifth century again reacted by adopting new weight standards: at Abdera and Maroneia the Aeginetan standard; at Thasos, Neapolis and Aenus the so-called 'Chian' system, with tetradrachms of about 15.6 grammes, together with drachms and smaller denominations. New types also began to appear: at Thasos (**145**), for instance, the old nymph and satyr design disappeared and was replaced by a head of Dionysus, accompanied on the reverse by a figure of Heracles drawing a bow. Fashion again is evident; at Aenus the head of Hermes is now depicted facing.

And what of Athens' former allies in the eastern Aegean? As in the north, the Attic standard was abandoned, mostly in favour of the Chian, though later the Persian weight standard became the most popular. Other trends we have encountered elsewhere are again evident: the inclusion of officials' names in the designs, changes of types (at some, but by no means at all, of the old mints), the use of a head as the standard obverse type, occasional production of gold coins, the first appearance of bronzes, and so on.

One of the most important fourth century mints was that of the city of Rhodes, a new capital founded jointly in 407 BC by the three old cities of the island of Rhodes, Camirus, Lindus and Ialysus. For its coinage the new city adopted the Chian standard. In fact, the term 'Rhodian' has in modern times been applied to this standard because of the very large issues of Rhodian coins. For its coin designs Rhodes (**146**) used a head of Helios (sometimes facing) and a rose, the flower from which the island took its name and which now became the official badge of the island. The rose now appears constantly on the coinage and is also to be found stamped on the handles of amphorae containing the famous Rhodian wine which travelled to all parts of the Greek world (*see* **Fig. 8**).

Rhodes was one of the cities involved in the alliance of cities from the eastern Aegean, who apparently once made an agreement to share production of an issue of coinage. This was the Σ Y N coinage already mentioned in chapter 4. Each city in the alliance identified itself with an

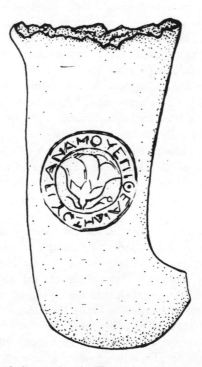

Fig. 8 *Rhodian amphora handle, third to second centuries* BC

appropriate reverse design, such as the rose for Rhodes and the bee for Ephesus (**147**), but they all used the same obverse type depicting the child Heracles strangling snakes, presumably symbolizing the alliance over-coming the evil of an oppressor. The date of this coinage is disputed: it has been identified both with a pro-Spartan alliance at the end of the Peloponnesian War and an anti-Spartan alliance from the period before the Peace of Antalcidas in 387 BC.

In the Ionian region two of the fifth century's major coin producers, Chios (**148**) and Samos, continued to issue in large quantities in the fourth century. The same coin types as before were retained, but both mints now included the names of officials within the designs and also produced issues of bronze coinage as well as the usual silver. A mint of growing importance in Ionia was Ephesus. The city had been issuing silver coinage from a very early date, but before 400 BC production was largely confined to small denominations. In the fourth century, however, a major series of tetradrachms (**149**) on the Chian weight standard was issued. The bee type used on earlier issues was retained for the obverse, but was now coupled with a design for the reverse showing the forepart of a stag and a palm tree, together with an official's name.

In the north-eastern Aegean major mints of the fourth century included Cyzicus which also, in addition to its electrum coins, now issued Chian-weight silver tetradrachms (**150**), and the two cities of Byzantium and Calchedon, facing each other across the Bosporus, which apparently cooperated in producing similar coinages. Both mints shared the same basic designs of a standing cow on the obverse and an old-fashioned stippled incuse square on the reverse, but each city was identified on the obverse with an abbreviated mint signature and a symbol underneath the cow: a dolphin for Byzantium and a corn ear for Chalchedon (**151**).

A few issues of gold coinage from the eastern Aegean have been dated to the first half of the fourth century. Teos in Ionia produced gold fractions at the beginning of the century and again in the 360s, when the nearby city of Clazomenae (**152**) probably issued its beautiful gold staters depicting a facing head of Apollo on the obverse and a swan on the reverse, accompanying silver tetradrachms with similar designs. Cius in the north produced a short series of gold later in the century, as also did the city of Panticapaeum (**252**) across the Black Sea in the Crimea. However, apart from the Persian darics, the most important gold coinage of the region, and indeed the only gold coinage issued on a regular basis before the time of Philip II of Macedon, was that of the city of Lampsacus (**153**). The gold staters of Lampsacus were struck to the same weight standard as the Persian darics and, like the darics, they travelled widely. An inscription from Thebes records that Byzantium contributed five hundred and eighty four Lampascene gold staters to the

Boeotians during the Sacred War of 356–346 BC. The Lampsacene gold is another of those coinages, like the electrum of Cyzicus, Phocaea and Mytilene, which used changing designs (on the obverse to accompany the standard Pegasus forepart on the reverse). Many of the designs are copied from the coins of other Greek cities, and some are notably well-executed and attractive.

One of the most significant developments in monetary history in the fourth century was the spread of bronze coinage (*see* chapter 6). We have seen how bronze coinage began in the second half of the fifth century in Sicily and south Italy. Another region where bronze coinage made an early start was the northern shore of the Black Sea, where the city of Olbia was already, in the fifth century, issuing cast bronze coins. Instead of conventional round pieces, Olbia at first also issued bronze money cast into the shapes of dolphins (**154**). Earlier, the region had apparently used bronze arrow heads as money.

In prehistoric Greece, various objects made of bronze or other base metals had been used as currency and there was an ancient tradition of cast iron money, a tradition which is represented by the famous spits (*oboloi*) found in excavations in the Temple of Hera at Argos. Ultra-conservative Sparta was still using iron spits as currency as late as the fourth century BC, but by this time production of struck bronze coinage was already widespread in the region. The first datable bronze coins from mainland Greece were issued by King Archelaus I of Macedon (413–399 BC). Thasos was another early producer of bronze coins, and by the middle of the fourth century issues were being struck at numerous mints in Macedonia, Thrace, Thessaly and the Peloponnese. Meanwhile, in the eastern Aegean Chios (**148**) and Samos began issuing their extensive series of bronze coins towards the end of the fifth or early in the fourth century, and many other issues from, for example, Lampsacus in the north and Caria and Lycia in the south, can be dated within the first half of the fourth century.

The Persian Empire

Asia Minor was one of the Persian Empire's frontier regions. Following the Greeks' victories of the 470s BC, the Persian grip on western Asia Minor was loosened and by the middle of the fifth century most of the cities and peoples of the coastal area had joined the Delian League. Even cities deep in Persian territory, such as Sinope in the north and Aspendus and Celenderis in the south, were at some time subscribers to the League, as also was Cyzicus, situated not far from Dascylium, the capital of one of the satrapies of Asia Minor. Similarly, the cities and kingdoms of Caria and Lycia, though listed within the provinces of the Persian Empire, were also for a time allies of Athens.

Uncertainties concerning the political allegiance of many cities and peoples in Asia Minor in the fifth century create real difficulties for any attempt at interpreting the coinages they produced and placing them in a relationship with the 'imperial' Persian darics and sigloi. However, there is absolutely no doubt that local issues of coinage were produced within the Persian Empire, proving that there was certainly no ban on local coinage, or at least no universal, effective ban. When the Athenian statesman Themistocles sought refuge at the Persian court in the 460s, following his ostracism from Athens, Artaxerxes I granted him some local revenues in western Asia Minor and some lands to govern there. He settled in Magnesia and there struck coins in his own name (**156**). A rare silver fraction recently identified as a coin of Themistocles from Magnesia even has a bearded portrait of the great man, making it by far the earliest datable portrait coin.

Other early portraits can be seen on the coins of Lycian dynasts from the later fifth and early fourth centuries, and also on coins issued by Persian satraps in Asia Minor. In fact, nearly all examples of portraits on coins that can be dated before the time of Alexander the Great seem to have been produced in the Persian Empire. The first Lycian dynast to be portrayed on a coin was Kharai, who ruled in the late fifth century. One of the coins on which his rather stylized portrait appears (**157**) has on the other side a head of Athena that is a direct copy of the head on fifth century Athenian coins.

The earliest portraits of Persian satraps began to appear slightly later, towards the very end of the fifth century. Amongst the most famous examples are a head on a coin of Cyzicus (**158**) signed Pharnabazus, which is thought to identify the well-known satrap of Dascylium (413–370 BC) and the head usually, but probably mistakenly, identified as a portrait of Tissaphernes, satrap of Sardes and a leading figure in the later stages of the Peloponnesian War, which appears on the so far unique silver tetradrachm (**159**) with a reverse design depicting an owl accompanied by the letters BAΣ for *Basileos* (the Great King of Persia). This design is again based on contemporary Athenian coins, but with the letters BAΣ instead of AΘE identifying the different authority behind the issue.

The BAΣ tetradrachm was found in a hoard from Karaman in Turkey, discovered in 1946, which was otherwise composed entirely of Athenian tetradrachms, though many of the 'owls' were eastern imitations rather than authentic tetradrachms from the mint of Athens. The large numbers of Athenian coins found in Asia Minor and further east, the widespread adoption of Athenian coin designs on eastern issues (**159, 161-4**), and indeed the production in the provinces of the Persian Empire of straight copies of Athenian coins (**160**), such as those found in the Karaman hoard, all clearly indicate that Athenian currency continued to circulate widely in the Persian Empire through the fifth and fourth centuries. The late continuation of this phenomenon is confirmed by the existence of 'owls' signed by Persian satraps (**162**) in the time of Alexander and also by an 'owl' bearing the name of King Artaxerxes III (358-337 BC) in Egyptian Demotic script (**161**).

Returning to Asia Minor we find that in the fifth century most of the local issues produced in Persian territories were concentrated in the western edges of the Empire, in the Greek cities of the coastal area, and in Lycia and Caria, where the local dynasts issued extensive coinages through the fifth and well into the fourth century. However, the most important coins produced in this region were the 'imperial' gold darics (**165**) and silver sigloi (**166**). The early development of the 'archer' type, which gave its name to these coins has already been described in chapter 3. The king with bow and spear design was retained after 479 BC and indeed remained in use through the fourth century, eventually being employed on the gold double darics issued in Babylonia from the time of Alexander the Great. In the meantime though, a fourth 'archer' type had appeared, showing the king with a short sword or dagger in addition to the usual bow (**166**). This type, which was mostly confined to silver sigloi, was introduced around 450 BC, was still in use in the fourth century and again reappeared on Alexander's double darics. It is noticeable that irregular-shaped flans of metal were often used for the 'dagger' sigloi which, together with the fact that they overlap in date with the 'spear' coins, suggests that they were struck at a second mint. The fifth century 'spear' archers, having descended in an apparently unbroken line from the 'Croeseids', are presumed to have been struck at Sardes; perhaps the 'dagger' coins were minted in another satrapy in Asia Minor, for instance Dascylium. In the fourth century greater differences in style suggest that several separate mints may have struck occasional issues.

Fractions of the 'spear' and 'dagger' silver sigloi are virtually non-existent. Such concentration on a single denomination suggests that this 'Persian' silver was not intended to be a flexible coinage, but was designed for a limited function, though of course output was immense. Similarly, gold coinage was almost entirely confined to a single denomination, the daric, weighing about 8.4 grammes. Circulation of silver sigloi was largely confined to Asia Minor, but the darics, being almost the only gold coins available anywhere in the fifth century and having few rivals in the fourth century, found their way to virtually every corner of the Mediterranean and the Near East. These were essentially the silver and gold coins of the Persian Empire's western satrapies in Asia Minor; in other words, in areas where there was regular contact with coin-using peoples, especially Greeks. One of their uses was in making payments to Greeks. The Spartan King Agesilaus noted wryly that he had been driven out of Asia in 394 BC by the 'archers' used by the Persians as bribes to incite opposition to Sparta in Greece.

After about 400 BC a definite decline in output of Persian sigloi is visible, though it seems there was no parallel fall in daric production; indeed, most of the surviving specimens of gold darics seem to date from the late fifth and, especially, the fourth century. The reason for the decline of the siglos is unclear, but it may perhaps be linked with a corresponding increase in production of other silver coinages within the Persian Empire.

In western Asia Minor in the fourth century we have already seen an upsurge in coining activity in the coastal Greek cities; and some of these cities, notably Clazomenae, were explicitly stated to be Persian possessions. Inland, the dynasts of Lycia continued to produce their regular issues of silver coinage. A Lycian (**167**) version of the fashion for facing heads as coin designs can be seen on the portrait coins of the dynast Pericles (380-362 BC), who also issued Lycia's first bronze coins (**168**). The Carian dynasts also coined throughout this period. The anonymous issues of the fifth century, which displayed local winged deities and curious pyramidal cult objects, thought to be sacred stones, sometimes accompanied by letters in local Carian script, were replaced in the fourth century by the issues of Hecatomnus (395-377 BC), Maussolus (**169**) (377-353 BC), and the other dynasts of the Hecatomnid dynasty, who ruled Caria for most of the century. The Hecatomnid coins are more Greek in character; their designs copied Greek coin types, such as the facing Apollo head from Rhodian coins, and they included issues in gold and bronze as well as silver.

After 400 BC the region of Cilicia in south-eastern Turkey became a quite important producer of coinage. The eastward advance of coin minting along the south coast of Turkey reached the Cilician cities of Celenderis and Tarsus (**171**) before the end of the fifth century, then, from about 400 BC, many more cities began striking. The major denomination produced at every city was the double siglos but small silver fractions were also issued in great quantities. Attractive designs were used, mostly copied from or based on the designs of other circulating coins. Some issues were signed by the cities, other issues were produced in the name of the satrap. There are examples of cities issuing both civic and satrapal coins apparently quite close together. Tarsus was the capital of the satrapy of Cilicia and the principal mint for the Cilician issues of the satraps Pharnabazus and Datames who, in the period 379-363 BC, produced a series of issues of double sigloi and silver fractions. One coinage (**172**), issued by both satraps, depicts a facing female head, which is clearly descended from the facing Arethusa by Kimon on the coinage of Syracuse, and on the reverse the bearded head of a warrior, perhaps representing the satrap himself. On some examples the helmet of the warrior is decorated with laurel leaves, showing that it is an adaptation of the Athena head on the ubiquitous Athenian 'wreathed' owls.

The Cilician issues of Pharnabazus and Datames were struck while these satraps were mobilising their forces for an attack on Egypt, and the earlier issues of Tiribazus (386–380 BC) were produced during preparations for an invasion of Cyprus, which was then, like Egypt later, in rebellion. In fact most satrapal coinages from this period can be linked with military activity, including further issues struck during the 360s when a number of the satraps of Asia Minor, including Datames, went into revolt against the Great King.

The steady advance of coinage into the Persian Empire did not stop in Cilicia. Cyprus had been issuing coinage since the archaic period, and the island's city-kingdoms continued to coin through the fifth and fourth centuries, adopting in the course of time new developments already seen elsewhere, such as production of gold and bronzes. On the nearby Phoenician coast the important cities of Sidon and Tyre began striking coinage in the period 450–425 BC. These first coins from the Levantine coastlands were soon followed by others and by the early fourth century numerous issues were appearing throughout the region. The coins of the kings of Sidon are interesting for illustrating the political situation of this region. They have designs which are purely Achaemenid: large pieces depict the Great King of Persia driven in a chariot and attended by a figure in Egyptian dress (**174**); smaller silver coins show a crowned figure slaying a lion (**175**) in a composition, with both figures upright, that is identical to designs on Achaemenid royal seals.

Another important coinage from this region is the so-called 'Philisto-Arabian' produced at Gaza and probably elsewhere in Palestine and neighbouring areas. On this coinage, which mainly consisted of small silver fractions, typically Achaemenid designs are again evident, but Greek coin designs were also copied, notably owls (**164**). This series includes the famous 'Yehud' coin (**176**), which has a bearded, helmeted head on the obverse and on the reverse a deity seated on a winged disc, accompanied by the word 'Judaea' in Aramaic script, which has been interpreted as an Achaemenid representation of the god of the Jews. The Philisto-Arabian series as a whole can be dated to the first half of the fourth century BC.

Finally, on the southern shore of the Mediterranean we have seen that Cyrenaica was issuing coinage in the archaic period, and through the fifth and most of the fourth century the coinage of the Cyrenaican cities continued along the lines already established. Cyrenaican coinage apparently made no impact on Egypt, further along the coast. The earliest coins that can be attributed to Egypt are issues of imitation Athenian owl tetradrachms, which were being produced in Memphis from the late fifth century. Other noteworthy issues include a gold stater with Athenian designs struck in the name of the Pharaoh Tachos while in rebellion against the Great King in the 360s, and also the 'hieroglyphic' gold stater of the Pharaoh Nectanebo II (177) already mentioned in chapter 4.

CHAPTER 6

Coinage in use

Coins in precious metal could be used for transactions of various sorts, or could be stored as wealth against the day on which they might be required. In this they differed not at all from the precious metal ingots that had preceded them as a medium for transactions and valuations, but the division into denominations, accurately produced to be as small as an eighth of an obol (0.08 gramme) (**112**), or as large as a gold forty-drachma piece (168 grammes) (**282**), created a flexible and practical monetary system on which the increasingly complex economy of the Greek world could be based.

Coining at a profit

The earliest recorded function of coins derives from their presence in the foundation deposit of the archaic temple of Artemis at Ephesus (**1-4**), where their role was that of a donative offered to the goddess and sealed below her temple. At about the same time, a hoard of very similar electrum coins was secreted in a pot at Colophon in Ionia, and on this occasion it would seem that the owner had hidden them in a safe place but had died without revealing their location to his family. The coins that had been put aside for safe-keeping lay there until recovered by chance in modern times. The earliest reference to coinage in literature, which must refer to a time not long after the foundation deposit was closed at Ephesus and the pot containing a man's savings was hidden at Colophon, records that two thousand staters, almost certainly in coin, were given to the poet-statesman Alcaeus by the Lydian king for military purposes in the early sixth century (*Alcaeus* frag. D. 11). King Croesus of Lydia gave two staters each to all the male citizens of Delphi (*Herodotus* I. 54) to ensure a favourable response from the oracle of Apollo about 550 BC.

Offerings, wealth, urgent payments and bribes are all uses to which coins
have been put ever since, but here they are documented from the earliest
period of the new medium.

The viability of coinage as a circulation medium relies on the trust that
all parties have in it. Coins are acceptable in return for goods or services
only insofar as they can be reused by the new owner without
unreasonable restriction. Coins of precious metal obviously have
advantages in inspiring confidence amongst the public that base metal
coins and paper money do not. It is becoming very clear that in ancient
times some coinages were not widely acceptable outside the area in
which they were made. The main reason for this was that they were
valued by those who issued them at a rate in excess, sometimes much in
excess, of their real bullion value. Indeed, this seems to be one of the
main reasons for the introduction of coins in the first place. The issuer
could increase the purchasing power in goods or services of a given batch
of metal by turning it into coins. For two generations only the gold/silver
alloy of electrum was used for coinage. Electrum had a recognised value
of its own as a separate precious metal. As a result, once the technology of
extracting the separate metals from natural electrum was mastered,
electrum could be made artificially. The quantity of gold could be
drastically reduced in the alloy without affecting the value at which the
coin would circulate. Satisfactory profits would thus accrue to the issuer
of the coins.

It is also a recognized phenomenon at a later date that some silver
coinages were remarkably restricted in their circulation. While the coins
of Athens at all periods are regularly found far from Attica, in the Near
East and in southern Italy many coinages are not found outside their
immediate geographical location. This often coincides with the
overstriking of coins from outside the area (**57, 133**) and with a tendency
for hoards to be composed mainly of coins from a limited area close to the
place of deposit, occasionally accompanied by a major currency from
outside the region. This pattern is, for example, common in Crete,
Sicily and Italy. There can be no doubt that a major reason for limited
circulation is that a coinage could be significantly more valuable within
the area of its origin than outside.

The overstriking of foreign coin enabled the state to fix a value for the
piece considerably in excess of its original value, so that the valuable
silver, imported in the form of coinage of another state, could be retained
within the territory of the issuing city. Merchants and private individuals
could lose considerably in the purchasing power of their coins if they
took them far from the city of origin. Economic zones were consciously
created in this way, particularly in areas which did not have ready access
to silver. The remarkable fifth century BC silver coinages of Syracuse

and other Sicilian states are very rarely found outside the island. It is certain that they played no part in the currency circulation of south Italy, and coins of Italy were not to be found in Sicily until the advent of the Roman denarius.

In the Hellenistic period, Ptolemy I of Egypt reduced the weight of his royal tetradrachm, the most common coin in circulation, and for the next three hundred years the Ptolemaic kings retained a close control over the coinage which they allowed to circulate within the kingdom. This is in stark contrast to the late archaic period, when Egypt readily absorbed the coinages of the Aegean area. At that time it seems clear that the value of silver in the Near East and Egypt was much higher than in the Aegean basin, where new mines of silver-bearing lead ores were being exploited. There was a vast increase in the quantity of silver available to those fortunate enough to possess such mines, and although the Persian governors did not think fit to issue a coinage at Memphis in Egypt until the fourth century, the coins of the Greek cities of the Aegean provided silver as a form of bullion from the late sixth century onwards.

In the second century, about 175 BC, the Attalid kings of Pergamum introduced a reduced weight royal coinage, which became known from the design of the cista mystica as a cistophorus (**259**), and this circulated within the kingdom side by side with coins of full Attic weight struck by free cities in the area (**258**). However, because the cistophori contained so much less silver than the Attic tetradrachms, the latter were much to be preferred for savings, and the hoards tend to be of one type of currency or the other, and not of the two mixed together. The heavier weight Attic tetradrachms also circulated into the Seleucid kingdom of Syria, while the cistophori remained firmly within the Attalid kingdom.

Drachma, obol and coin denominations

Weight is an essential element in coinage of precious metals, and the names chosen for the basic coin denominations reflect this. The terms 'obol' and 'drachma' are the most commonly recorded denominations. Six obols always equalled a drachma. Traditionally it has been assumed that the obol was the basic unit of currency. This is based on the fact that the obol derived its name from the Greek *obelos*, meaning an iron spit. There is convincing authority from ancient times that these simple cooking utensils were used as a currency medium, as were tripods, cauldrons and other metal implements. Coins of cast iron have survived from Argos and other central Greek mints, and there are reported to be such pieces from Byzantium and Clazomenae. The derivation of the coin term obol from spits therefore seems most plausible, and it is assumed that iron spit and silver obol were directly related as equivalent in value. The Greek word *drax*, meaning a handful, is the origin of the term drachma, and is thus believed to have signified a handful of spits (obols). 'Six iron spits were as many as the hand could conveniently grasp' (*Kraay*, 1976).

Such an explanation of the derivation of the obol as the sixth of the drachma is not as simple as is currently believed. From the existing coins it is clear that the actual weight of the drachma differed significantly from place to place, according to the weight standard in use. At Athens the drachma was a little over four grammes (**109**), and the obol was thus 0.65 gramme (**111**). At Aegina the drachma was nearly 50 per cent heavier, over six grammes (**33**), and the obol was over one gramme (**34**). At Corinth the drachma was less than half that at Aegina, at 2.85 grammes (**43**), and the obol was consequently less than half a gramme (**44**). If the obol was really the basic unit of currency, this very considerable variation in terms of its value in silver, within such a small geographical area, must be properly explained, and no explanation has been offered. With the obol at Aegina being more than twice that at Corinth, it would seem very unlikely indeed that the same single object could really be represented in silver at the two places. To suggest that the Corinthians were using a small spit as their unit and the Aeginetans a large one is an hypothesis that could be further explored, but is rather unlikely. The weight of the coins was in all cases probably less than the commercial weight of bullion silver, and it could be suggested that the coins of Athens and Corinth were simply much lighter in relation to the commercial drachma and obol than the coins of Aegina. However, we know from commercial weights which have been found inscribed with their coin equivalents that at Athens the difference was only some 5 per cent. Indeed, the desirability of Athenian and Corinthian coins outside their area of origin, testified by their circulation and in ancient literature, preclude any possibility that the Aeginetan drachmae and obols were any closer to their bullion value. There are different weight standards at the three cities, and the idea that the obol was the basic unit on which all the weight standards were based is an oversimplification of reality.

In Sicily the *litra* represented a pound weight of bronze, and this was used as a unit of money. As coinage, this had a regular conversion into silver at a little below the weight of the Aeginetan obol, and the fractions of the litra (*unciae*) are even marked on the rare fractional silver coins issued in the fifth century BC (**76**). The coins of Syracuse that are known today as decadrachms (**81-2**) are in reality fifty-litra pieces (*Diodorus* XI.26.3), and the local and Greek weight systems are thus assimilated in the coinage. In this case there is no doubt of the origin of the coin denomination, and it is based on a unit of weight, not on the accepted value of an object.

In Greece it is important to recognize the universal acceptance that the obol should be a sixth of a drachma. To the east, in the electrum and early silver coinage of Asia Minor, we find that the sixth was a regular fraction of the stater, and the sexagesimal system of division, which makes the sixth a natural fraction, can be traced back to earliest times. It makes a great deal more sense to consider the drachma to be the basic unit, of which the sixth became universally known as an obol, as a nickname. In the same way, when bronze coinage was introduced, the term *chalkous* ('bronze') was used first as a nickname, like the English 'copper', and then the name became adopted as a denomination. The terms *dichalkon* and *tetrachalkon* were culled as multiples in the same way as the *diobol* and *tetrobol*.

If the drachma was the basic unit, there is no need to continue the myth that the 'handful' represented six spits. Rather, the 'handful' should be recognized as a natural weight in its own right, and a handful of grain, a natural unit of weight adopted in other places and at other times, could be of sufficiently different weight from place to place to create significantly differing weight standards. When fractions came to be adopted as coinage, the term obol was applied to sixths, referring indeed to a time when spits were used as a term of valuation, but without the need to equate the sixth with the exact value of a spit.

Therefore the basis of the terms drachma and obol is the traditional weight system of individual city states. These could vary considerably in weight. A change in the weight standard used for the coins is often apparent amongst the issues of a single city, caused, perhaps, by changes in political or economic affiliation (Byzantium and Calchedon, *see* chapter 8). This is familiar to the citizens of Great Britain who have recently experienced the change from pounds and ounces to kilogrammes and grammes, but the pattern of weight standards of ancient Greek coins may appear extremely complicated at first sight. Since the weights used for coinage were generally somewhat lighter than the commercial weights used in the market place (*see* **Fig.4**), the terms adopted by numismatists in the nineteenth century make the picture even more confusing. 'Light' or 'reduced' Attic weight, for example, may be used for a series which does not conform fully to the weight system that is known as the Attic standard. This probably indicates that the state had purposefully chosen a slightly lighter standard for the coin, with even greater reduction from the commercial standard, in order thereby to increase the profits obtained from striking a coinage.

Profit was not the only reason for choosing a strange standard. The weight of a silver coin may be geared specifically to the exchange ratio between gold and silver. At Sardes, gold and silver coinage (**13-14**) began on the same weight standard, with a stater of 10.65 grammes. Since the normal ratio of silver to gold was 13⅓:1, this caused problems in the exchange of the two metals. The gold stater was therefore reduced in weight, to 8.2 grammes, to allow ten of the staters in silver to pass for the one gold stater. The introduction of the daric with the Persian archer type (**17**) saw a slight increase in the weight of the gold piece to 8.4 grammes, with the silver 'siglos' continuing the weight of the earlier half stater. The daric was in fact close in weight to the Babylonian shekel, whereas the siglos, the name of which was a Greek form of the word shekel, was of a weight that reflected no shekel weight. It was a nickname which, like the 'obol', owed its origin to common parlance without reflecting the academic derivation of its weight. The convenience of practical handling had here influenced the choice of weight for the daric. As a result, the double 'siglos' (stater) came to be widely used in areas under Persian domination, representing as it did the tenth of the daric.

Exchange between standards must have been a regular problem for anyone with dealings outside his own city. The inscription listing the accounts of the building of the temple of Asclepius at Epidaurus shows how a city using the Aeginetic standard (**130**) accounted for purchases from Athens, where prices were all quoted using the Attic standard. In about 375 BC six hundred Attic drachmae had to be paid for marble from the quarries on Mount Pentelikon. The ratio of the weight of the Aeginetic to that of the Attic drachma was 7:10, and so four hundred and twenty Aeginetic weight drachmae were paid, but twenty five further drachmae were added on to cover the commission required by the moneychangers. This works out at just over 10 per cent, or one obol per Attic tetradrachm. Such commissions were a common requirement when exchanging between different currencies, or when changing between gold, silver or bronze. In Ptolemaic Egypt exchange of copper for silver is regularly quoted in papyri, for example in payments of taxes demanded in silver but actually paid in bronze coins. The commission here is normally 10 per cent, and the state permitted the bankers to levy it.

Coinage in circulation

To those unaccustomed to using coins in precious metal it may seem surprising that the currency in circulation in a particular place could be composed of coins from many different origins. There is a tendency to think of the issuing of money for circulation as being a symbol of an independence jealously guarded by the state. However, it was commonplace in the ancient Greek world for a variety of coinages to be found in circulation, as indeed it was in seventeenth and eighteenth century Europe, where traders had books to enable them to determine the comparative value of the coins likely to pass through their hands and scales to weigh them.

In the archaic period it was the value of the silver and the convenience of the coined unit which caused wide circulation from the area of issue. In later times certain coinages, which had gained a trustworthy reputation, were deemed to be officially acceptable far from the city of origin and without, necessarily, any political implications. Athenian coin with its reputation for purity came to be widely accepted in the East and had a remarkable influence. In Babylonia, the Great King of Persia issued no coins of his own, although in the western satrapy of Sardes the royal Achaemenid coinage played a significant role for two centuries. The coinage of Babylonia under Archaemenid rule consisted of imitations of Athenian tetradrachms in the fourth century BC, indistinguishable from the original except in style (**160**). In the satrapy of Egypt the same phenomenon occurred. It has recently been recognized that the mint of Memphis became a major producer of 'Athenian' coins in the mid-fourth century. On one occasion (*c*.343 BC) an issue was inscribed in Demotic Egyptian, the name of King Artaxerxes replacing the initial letters of the name of the Athenians (**161**). Towards the end of the Persian period the satraps of Egypt placed their own names on the coins. In Lycia and Palestine there was similar influence of the Athenian 'owl' coinage, representing as the designs did 'good money'.

At Athens itself an inscription discovered in 1970, which may be dated to *c*.375 BC, shows how a city could settle problems of the acceptance of currency that arose from day to day. This is a law prescribing that under pain of severe penalty officials should be appointed to be at a certain spot near the bankers' area in the market place, whenever business was being contracted, and in the harbour area of the Peiraeus, in order to solve disputes concerning the acceptability of particular coins. All coinage stamped with official Athenian designs had to be accepted unless it could be shown that a particular piece was of poor silver or was plated with a silver coating on a copper core. Such pieces were to be at once withdrawn from circulation, cut to declare their invalidity and placed for safe keeping in the Metroon, under the responsibility of the Boule (Council). The official, needed to have enough experience to decide what was and was not acceptable, and his main concern may well have been for the pieces of small denomination used in daily transactions. In the unlikely event that Egyptian or Babylonian imitations were to find their way to the Athenian agora, it would be his decision as to whether they should be allowed to pass into circulation. It is to be presumed that an official of this nature could distinguish these pieces and that such imitations would not be regarded as of Athenian origin.

Foreign coins proffered in Athens were not to be confiscated but were to be returned to the owner. Since here and elsewhere it was the city's own coinage that was legal tender, the owner of foreign coin could either change his coins at the bankers' tables or he could barter for their use in private negotiation. Hoards of coins which have survived show that it was quite normal at all periods for an individual to hold silver coins from many different sources, and the official accounts of the cities, inscribed in stone, show the same phenomenon.

The one inscription to survive providing accounts connected with the minting of coins comes from Delphi, (c.336 BC). This lists the weights of coins melted down to provide the metal for the new Amphictionic Council issue (182), and it shows the variety of central Greek coinages that had reached the treasury in large quantities.

At Delos in the second century BC, the origins of the coinage deposited in the treasury of the sanctuary of Apollo are carefully recorded year by year, each pot in which they were stored listed separately. These inscriptions are extremely useful, both for the coins circulating at Delos during the period and for the names by which the coins were known in common parlance. Some of these, like the cistophorus (259), mentioned above, have passed into use in modern times, and most of the terms are immediately recognizable from surviving coins. The New Style silver coinage of Athens, with the design on the reverse bordered by a wreath of olive, were simply called 'stephanephori', 'bearing wreath' (241-4), the late drachmae of Rhodes with shallow incuse square were termed 'plinthophori', 'bearing plinth' (266). Some of the names remain of doubtful origin. The gold 'tettiges' 'cicadas' may represent a coin that has not survived. The 'new taurophori silver tetradrachms' may be the coins of the First Macedonian Republic which were issued for a short time in 168/7 BC, and depict the cult image of Artemis Taurophoros (Artemis carried on a bull) from her sanctuary at Amphipolis. However, there are other possibilities, such as the fine tetradrachms of Eretria in Euboea, of similar date with reverse bull in wreath.

In most states, particularly where it was important to protect the circulation of local silver coinage, a law could be enacted stipulating that all payments should be made in the state's own currency. Such a law has survived from Olbia in south Russia, datable to the fourth century BC. Here, import and export of struck gold and silver coin was not restricted, but all sales and purchases of such coins had to take place 'at the stone in the assembly building'. Within the city all purchases had to be made in the city's silver and bronze coinage. The official exchange rate was quoted for the Cyzicenes, stipulated to be ten and a half silver staters of Olbia (251). The Cyzicenes are known from fifth century Athenian inscriptions and elsewhere, and can be identified with large electrum

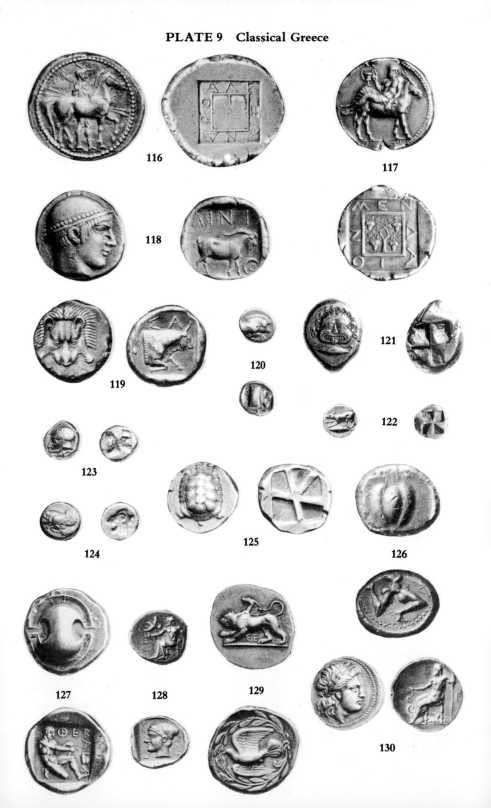

PLATE 9 Classical Greece

116

117

118

119

120

121

122

123

124

125

126

127

128

129

130

PLATE 10 Peloponnese, central Greece

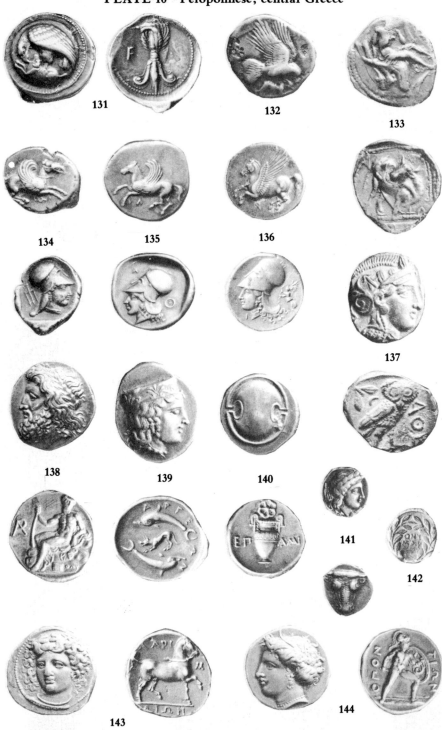

131

132

133

134

135

136

137

138

139

140

141

142

143

144

PLATE 11 North Greece, Black Sea, Persian Empire

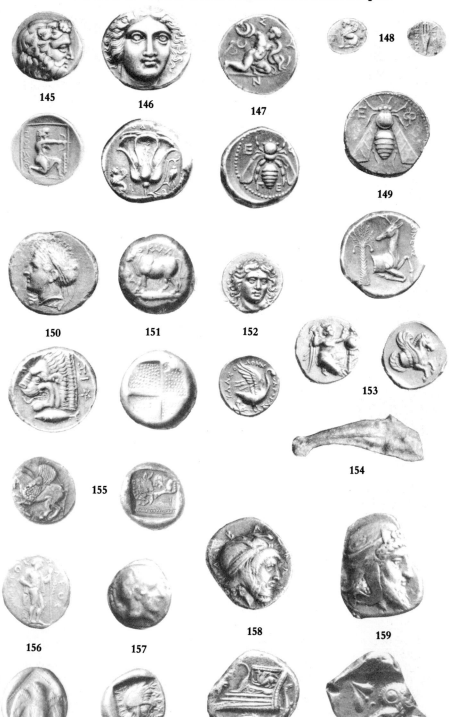

145

146

147

148

149

150 151 152

153

154

155

156 157 158 159

PLATE 12 Persian Empire

160

161

162

163

164

165

166

167

169

168

171

170

176

172

173

174

177

175

PLATE 13 Macedonia

178 179 180 181 182

183 184

185 186 187 188

189 190

PLATE 14 Alexander's empire

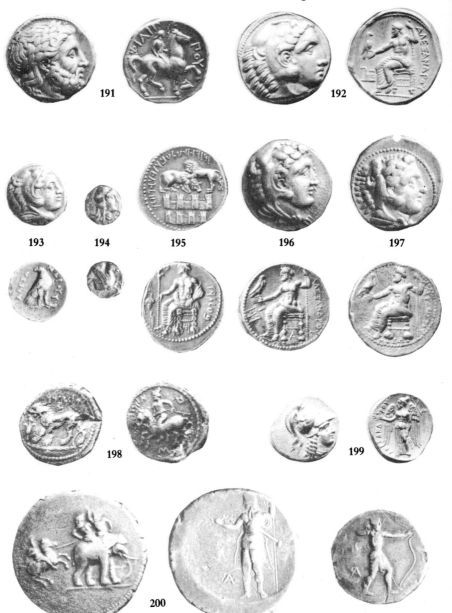

191

192

193   194   195   196   197

198   199

200   201

202

203

204

205

206

207

208

209

210

211

212

213

214

215

PLATE 16   Diadochi: Philip III, Seleucus I, Ptolemy I

216   217   218   219

220   221   222   223

225   226   227

224

coinage (*see* chapters 4 and 5), issued throughout the fifth and most of the fourth century BC, with designs that varied with every issue (**121-2**). The unifying features that show the issues to be from the same mint are the fabric and a tunny fish, a constant ancillary symbol that is used in every design. This device was the badge of the city of Cyzicus, but these coins were only recognized to be a single series in the mid-nineteenth century, and prior to that the many different designs were attributed to different cities. Similarly, what we now know as electrum was regularly called gold until the mid-nineteenth century, and it was no doubt as gold that these pieces were known to the Olbians.

The extraordinary nature of the Cyzicenes has not been fully explored. Although the electrum coins do not bear an ethnic, they were marked as coming from Cyzicus by the appearance of the tunny fish (*see* chapter 4). In the fourth century they were issued beside the city's own silver coinage which was inscribed with an ethnic (**150**). Unlike the silver coinage, the electrum coinage had a wide circulation in the Black Sea region and in Greece. Cyzicus lay in the Persian Empire, close to the satrapal seat of Dascylium, which controlled the northern part of Asia Minor. Dascylium itself is not known to have struck a coinage but, bearing in mind the flourishing darics and sigloi emanating from the Persian satrapy of Sardes, it seems very probable that the Persians used Cyzicene electrum as if it was a coinage for the satrapy. The Cyzicenes bore no ethnic. The electrum alloy of the staters may have been adjusted to allow the coins to pass at the same value as a daric with, perhaps, a slight overvaluation in favour of the purer metal. Pharnabazus, the Persian satrap of Dascylium, certainly used the mint of Cyzicus at which to strike a silver coinage in about 395 BC, with his portrait on the obverse (**158**), again without applying the ethnic to the reverse but with the identifying tunny fish in the design.

Also, from the early fourth century comes the decree mentioned in chapters 4 and 5 announcing co-operation between two states over the production of fractional electrum coinage. This too must be seen in the context of cities subject to the Persian Empire, but there is no suggestion in the inscription that the Great King or his satrap had any part in the organization of this monetary treaty between Phocaea on the coast of Asia Minor and Mytilene on the island of Lesbos. Both cities struck electrum sixth staters, which served as fractions of the daric in the Black Sea area, the equivalent of a silver tetradrachm on the Attic standard. The decree establishes that each city agreed to strike in alternate years but, more importantly, the quality of the alloy was also established and the death penalty was prescribed for an official convicted of adulterating the metal.

Malpractice

The profits that could be made by those responsible for the production of coinage were well-known to all. Aristotle mentions that small fragments of silver were ejected from blisters that formed on the surface of the metal as it began to cool from a molten state. This was in fact evidence of the metal's purity, the blisters being formed, as we know today, by the expulsion of oxygen in a silver that contains no more than 2-3 per cent impurity. The mint workers used to gather the pieces carefully and carry them off. Far more serious was the possibility of malpractice that could produce illicit gains at the expense of the state, and to the detriment of the general acceptability of the coinage. Hikesias of Sinope, father of the philosopher Diogenes, was, we are told, exiled from his city for such an offence. The adulteration of the silver by the addition of more lead or copper, plating with silver on a copper core, or simply the regular production of slightly lightweight silver pieces would all give a fair profit and the state had to provide safeguards.

The testing of the coinge in circulation must have been a daily occurrence in the Greek world. Chance has preserved for us the inscription, mentioned above, that describes the appointment for this purpose of an official at Athens. Such a person must have been required in most cities. In an Egyptian papyrus of about 260 BC we find that officials responsible for testing coins (*dokimastai*) were also used as debt collectors, presumably because their knowledge of the coins would save the creditor from being cheated. For gold the ordinary citizen had recourse to the touch stone, or the Lydian stone as it was known to the Greeks. By scratching the surface of the metal this allowed comparison of the colour with samples of known fineness, to provide a fairly accurate examination of the purity. For silver coins serious adulteration of the metal might have been visible to the wary eye, but plating on a copper core, which normally produced a lightweight coin, required a cut or punch to break through the surface and reveal the true nature of the piece. Simple chopping is commonplace up to the fourth century BC. Indeed it is normal to find hoards of Greek coins in the Near East, particularly of the archaic period, in which every piece is carefully chopped.

A somewhat more sophisticated method of testing was by stamping the coin with a small seal-like die, bearing a device which might identify the person who had carried out the test. Such a personal 'countermark' was used with the earliest electrum coinage (6), and was an effective method of testing the purity of the metal. It had the further advantage that the countermark, like the original die, could have the effect of a mark of guarantee. In the fifth and fourth centuries certain coinages, such as the staters of Elis (32), the sigloi of the Persians from western Asia Minor and the staters of Aspendus (**170**) in Pamphylia, attracted a plethora of such marks. In none of these cases did the coins travel far from the place of origin, and it is clear that it became fashionable for local traders or dignataries to add personal marks to provide some further guarantee for the circulation of the pieces.

Cities also adopted the countermark as a simple way of restriking an existing coinage to enable it to circulate freely within the area of the city's jurisdiction (**253**) (*see* chapter 8). Although even less elegant than the complete overstriking of the coin, this provided a quick method of putting 'new' coins into circulation. There are even cases in which pincer countermark dies were used, truly restriking the coin obverse and reverse, but with miniature dies far smaller than the flan of the coin itself (**255**). Countermarks on bronze coins often occurred at a time when there was some change in the size of denominations. A design taken from the later coinage was stamped upon the earlier examples to identify the equation as denominations of two coins different in size. Under the Roman Empire this was extended to the use of marks of value countermarked on the existing coins to revalue them as quickly as possible.

Bronze coinage

The introduction of bronze coinage was a practical response to the increasing use of coinage in all daily transactions. One indication of the greater part played by coinage in daily life comes from the practice of placing a coin, officially an obol, in the mouths of the dead. The reason was that in this way the dead person could pay the ferryman Charon to take him across the river Styx to the abode of the dead in Hades. Such an idea requires, of course, that such a payment was normal in life. The modern excavation of cemeteries shows that this burial custom only began in the latter part of the fifth century BC, and this ties in neatly with other evidence for the more general use of coins. The earliest reference in literature is in *The Frogs* of Aristophanes (404 BC) which may indeed be making comedy out of a new custom.

At Athens a payment of two obols a day was introduced in the mid-fifth century to recompense those required to exercise their democratic right by serving on juries. This was raised to three obols during the early part of the Peloponnesian War, and later a similar payment was introduced for attendance at the assembly. The bronze ticket given to each of the jurymen and inscribed with his name was also stamped with the owl of the city. **Figure 9** shows a broken specimen of such a ticket from the early fourth century BC, with the stamp clearly derived from the silver triobol (**110**) of the city's coinage. The valuation in coins of the

Fig. 9   *Athenian pinakion (voting ticket), late fifth to fourth century* BC

of a day's labour shows that at the time when the payments were introduced the economy at Athens was demanding the use of coins to an ever greater extent. Payment for service, such as the drachma a day awarded before 411 BC to those elected to the Council, was part of the same development. Indeed, democracy could hardly have flourished in the same way without the existence of coins of small value. With payment for service becoming more common, the use of coins in the marketplace and in transactions of all sorts increased considerably, with a consequent increase in the demand for pieces of small denomination. In the works of Aristophanes the new use of small coins was often an occasion to raise a laugh. It was customary to hold them in the mouth for safe-keeping, and in *The Wasps* (lines 790-1) Philocleon pops fish scales into his mouth, thinking that they are coins. When he goes home with his jury pay under his tongue, his daughter (lines 608-9) manages to get it away from him in a welcoming kiss! Euelpides (*The Birds* 503) swallows an obol by mistake. At Athens fractions of silver are known as small as the eighth of an obol (hemitetartemorion **112**), but it is also possible to trace the Athenians' reluctant progress towards a bronze coinage. In the mid-fifth century BC, at the very time that the payments for state service were introduced, one Dionysius proposed that a coinage in bronze should be put into circulation to replace the impractical small fractions in silver. The law failed to meet approval, and Dionysius gained the nickname 'copper' (Chalkous) as the indignant Athenians refused to sully the reputation that their fine silver coinage enjoyed.

Towards the end of the fifth century BC, with their silver mines in the hands of the Spartans the Athenians were forced to produce an emergency issue of gold and, later, drachmae and tetradrachms of copper plated with silver. It is probably at this time that the marketplace began to see small, bronze, coin-like pieces that have been found in the Agora excavations. These may have been private issues, since they display a great variety of designs, in contrast to the official coinage, and lack of any ethnic (**115**). There is rarely any connection between the design of these pieces, now known as 'kollyboi', and the rest of Athenian coinage.

Indeed we know of one issue made privately by an Athenian citizen. Timotheus, an Athenian general, issued a coinage of bronze when he was unable to pay his troops during his siege of Olynthus in the campaign against the Chalcidian League, (364-359 BC). This has been identified with a particular variety of Athenian coinage found during the excavations at Olynthus, which differs from all other Athenian issues of the Hellenistic period in having the inscription AΘH instead of the traditional archaic form AΘE (**179**). In this case we know from the anecdote preserved in the *Oeconomica* that Timotheus issued this coinage on his own initiative at a time of financial crisis, having first persuaded the local shopkeepers to accept his bronze coins on the promise to redeem them for silver at a later date. The coins believed to have been struck by Timotheus are marked with one or two dots, which presumably indicate that he intended them to pass at one or two obols. It is by no means impossible that traders in the Agora at Athens used similar private tokens to facilitate the conduct of daily business at a time when the state did not provide sufficiently practical low denominations of coinage. The final adoption of coinage in bronze at Athens was not until the third quarter of the fourth century BC, more than a hundred years after the pioneering proposal of Dionysius.

We know that Dionysius himself left Athens in 443 BC as one of the founders of the new colony as Thurii in Italy, and it is significant that Thurii was one of the first cities to adopt bronze coinage of a practical size, very soon after the foundation of the colony (**97**). At about the same time in Sicily, Acragas and Himera were beginning a more general move towards bronze coinage (**77-79**) to replace impractical fractions in silver (**80**), and this had spread across the island by the end of the century. Dionysius, inspired perhaps by their practical example, was determined to see the new medium brought into use.

The reluctance at Athens to accept bronze coins is echoed by an inscription from Gortyna in Crete at the end of the fourth century BC. Here, it was apparently the citizens who were reluctant to accept the bronze coinage that the city's council had put into circulation. The law insists that the new bronze coinage be accepted by all within the city as legal tender, under pain of a heavy fine. It was no doubt a common occurrence that the city had to take stern measures to govern the coinage in circulation. This inscription from Gortyna is the only one to survive which touches upon the problems in introducing a new coinage. The value at which the new bronze tokens were to circulate was sometimes marked on them, or could be understood from the designs. Dots were much used in early Sicilian bronze coins to indicate the number of unciae (**78-9**), and double or triple types could represent double or triple units. Normally the denominations were fractions of the obol, accounted in chalkoi, but at a late date high value bronze coins are found, such as the bronze drachmae at Byzantium and Melos.

Coinage in the city

Malpractice by individuals was as readily expected as malpractice by those in power whose imagination in methods of taxing the people was recorded in the fourth century in the *Oeconomica,* a work once attributed to Aristotle. Maussolus of Caria, famous today from his tomb the Maussoleum of Halicarnassus, was a past master at raising taxes. On one occasion, when he was pressed by the Great King of Persia to pay his tribute, he told the people of Mylasa that the Persians were threatening to invade and that they must quickly raise money to strengthen the city defences. The citizens were only too ready to subscribe, but Maussolus then announced that an oracle had forbidden the building of city walls at the present time and he used the money to pay the tribute.

Taxes of all sorts were a common occurrence in the Greek world. At Byzantium in the fourth century BC the state levied a tax of 10 per cent first on all profits made by traders in the Black Sea and then on all purchases made within the city (*Oeconomica* II.3). It has indeed been suggested that taxes played a major role in the development of coinage from metal by weight, since the units provided by coinage formed the ideal basis for measuring the tax required. Particular denominations of coins of a particular weight standard could be stipulated for payment on any occasion.

The prices of goods naturally fluctuated according to quality and the prevailing conditions in the market. Aristophanes makes the point in *The Peace* (line 1201*ff*). The maker of sickles says that the advent of the brief peace in 421 BC had made the price of sickles soar, while the maker of helmet crests complains that the peace has ruined him. An extremely useful guide to the prices in 415/4 BC is a group of inscriptions recording the sale of property confiscated from the statesman Alcibiades and others who had committed sacrilege and defiled the sacred mysteries of Eleusis. The average price for a slave was one hundred and seventy eight drachmae for a woman, or one hundred and seventy nine for a man. A child could be purchased for seventy two drachmae. By way of comparison, in the fourth century BC an exceptional courtesan could cost three thousand drachmae (*Demosthenes* LIX.29), and in the Roman period a slave might cost five hundred drachmae. Alcibiades' comfortable chair cost two drachmae one obol, a simple stool just over a drachma. To contrast this with earnings, a skilled mason at Athens working on the Erechtheum temple at about the same time was paid a drachma a day.

A sheep in the time of Solon cost a drachma (*Plutarch Solon* 23), but soon after 403 BC they were valued at twelve to seventeen drachmae. In 329/8 BC, a year of famine, a sheep at Eleusis is quoted at thirty drachmae. Inflation was a fact of life, and although moderate in most of the Hellenistic period there were periods of sharp rises of prices, particularly noticeable in Egypt in the second century BC, and inflation became thoroughly out of control under the Roman Empire. The effect on coinage was therefore not dramatic in the pre-Roman world. The tetradrachm continued to be the regular large size denomination, but the introduction of regular gold coinages in the fourth century BC made pieces of much higher purchasing power more readily available.

The state accounts inscribed in stone are a fruitful source of information of all sorts. The tribute paid by the members of the Delian Confederacy to Athens was carefully recorded year by year, showing the amount allotted for payment by each state in Attic drachmae and the amount actually paid, giving a remarkable contemporary picture of the Confederacy. With the arrival of the Romans in the second century BC little change took place locally, either in the coinage or in the accounting, and it was not until the time of Augustus that the Thessalian League, for example, turned from accounting in League staters to accounting in Roman denarii. Thereafter, the uniformity of the monetary system imposed by the Romans became ever more noticeable until Greek coinage ceased in the third century AD.

CHAPTER 7

Philip II, Alexander, and the creation of the Hellenistic monarchies

When Philip II ascended the throne of Macedon in 359 BC, he inherited a small state which, under his father Amyntas III, had suffered severely at the hands of the Chalcidian League of Greek cities. Archelaus (413–389 BC) had moved the capital from Aegae in the mountains to Pella on the plain, and Pella itself was even captured by the League for a time in the troubled years preceding the reign of Philip. The extraordinary transformation that Philip achieved in the political scene by conquering the Chalcidian League and drawing surrounding territories into the kingdom is well reflected in his coinage. Philip created the foundations for the dramatic expedition which his son, Alexander the Great, launched against the Persian Empire. By taking control of the gold and silver mines on which the economy of the Chalcidian League was based, and by actively prospecting for new sources of precious metal, Philip transferred the fragile economy of his predecessors into one firmly based on a rich and regular income. Amyntas III had been forced to resort to silver-plated tetradrachms and issues of poor alloy (**178**), in his vain attempt to repulse the Chalcidian League. Philip left a legacy of a rich coinage in gold and silver which his son would expand and exploit.

The significance of Philip II

While the rare issues of silver and bronze which comprised the coinage of Perdiccas III (365–359 BC) were of minor importance, there is little coinage that has been attributed to the first three years of Philip's reign in the recent study by Georges Le Rider. Until he established a firm control over the area to the east of Pella, Philip had no greater access to silver than did Perdiccas III. The capture of Amphipolis in 357/6 BC brought with it the acquisition of silver mines in the area of Mount Pangaeus. This was the turning point of Macedonian fortunes. Le Rider, in his painstaking die-linking of the gold and silver issues, found that there evolved two parallel sequences of issues which clearly represented separate mints striking at the same time. Following E.T. Newell's suggestion that Amphipolis, close to the mining area, was a major mint during the reign of Alexander the Great, Le Rider placed one of the sequences of coinage at Amphipolis starting in 357/6 BC, and the other at the capital, Pella.

Through his conquests to the east Philip acquired the area of Krenides, where the Thasians three years previously had begun to exploit a gold mine (**188**). It was here that Philip in 356 BC founded the town that was to bear his name, Philippi, and a short but vigorous coinage in gold and silver emanated from the city for a few years after its foundation (**189-90**).

The success in his military expeditions in Macedonia and Thrace soon made Philip a major figure in Greek politics. In 352 BC he was elected leader of the Thessalian Confederacy and was thus invited to settle internal disputes of the cities. Through the Amphictionic League at Delphi he was able to influence affairs throughout Greece. Finally in 338 BC, after opposition had been crushed at the battle of Chaironeia, delegates from all Greek states except Sparta were gathered at Corinth, and Philip's vision of a united Greek expedition to free the Greeks of Asia Minor from Persian rule became a reality and he, naturally, was elected the leader. The effect of Philip's policies on the city coinages of the Greeks was not, perhaps, as marked as has traditionally been believed. The coinage of Thebes almost certainly continued through this troubled period until the destruction of the city by Alexander in 335 BC. That of Corinth certainly flourished during the reign of Philip, and even the coinage of Larissa in Thessaly, whose leadership of the Confederacy was taken by Philip, is now believed to have continued well into the reign of Alexander.

It is usually believed that Philip exploited the gold resources of Mount Pangaeus to a great extent, and was able to equip his army on the proceeds for his various military expeditions against the Chalcidian League and other Greeks. The study of the coinage through the hoards and die links, however, revealed that very little of the gold coinage in the name of Philip appeared to belong to his lifetime. There can have been only a limited number of issues, and those relatively small. As with the silver, two sequences evolved in the gold coinage, and Le Rider concluded that these should also be attributed to Amphipolis and Pella, but only after the final defeat of the Chalcidian League and the destruction of Olynthus in 348 BC. Philip died in 336 BC, and it has to be assumed that Alexander continued the gold coinage in the name of Philip posthumously for several years.

The tradition has been preserved by Plutarch (*Alexander* 4) that Philip was personally responsible for the choice of his coin designs. He wished to commemorate through the coinage his victory in the Olympic games, and the victorious jockey carrying a palm, on the silver (**184**), and the two-horsed chariot, on the gold (**186**), are sufficient commentary on this story. A second design is used for the silver that depicts the king himself on horseback, raising his hand in salute, and some of these depict a ribbon attached to the horse's bridle, which is equally a symbol of victory (**183**).

There has been some dissent on the details of the chronology proposed by Le Rider, but three very important points of interest emerge for the understanding of the history of coinage. First, the striking of a coinage of the same designs in more than one place at the same time was something of an innovation. Precedents may be found in the coinage of Corinthian type, struck in colonies in north-west Greece and in Italy, and differing from the coinage of the mother city only in the accompanying letters and symbols. How far the authority for these issues was centralized we do not know, though they had a common purpose. The Persians opened a second mint in Asia Minor in the mid-fifth century BC (*see* chapter 5). The model provided by these and the alliance coinages of the Boeotians and elsewhere might have led Philip to open one mint at the point to which taxes were paid, the administrative capital Pella, and another in the area where silver and gold were being freshly mined, Amphipolis. Since this was the coinage of the king, there was no need to mark the city of issue, as had been done in the case of the Corinthian and Boeotian coinages. The subsidiary symbols were sufficient at the time of issue to designate who was responsible.

Regular issues of gold were also an innovation in Greece. The darics had of course poured from Sardes previously, and in Syracuse the issues of gold staters had been produced over a fair period of time in order to finance the defence of the city against the Carthaginians. Philip paved the way for his son and those later Hellenistic monarchs who came to have the need for a regular coinage in gold.

The concept of a posthumous coinage is a further innovation. As a precedent one might again quote the daric which continued the coinage begun by Darius I, and which adopted his name. The idea that a royal coinage inscribed with the name of a dead king should be struck alongside the new regal coinage of his successor is a novelty and requires some explanation.

Le Rider's arrangement may not fully survive the test of time in all details. It is certain that Philip III Arrhidaeus struck coinage of the same types as Philip II during his short reign from 323 to 317 BC (**187**). In reality these coin issues are the coinage of Philip III, and are not correctly titled posthumous issues of Philip II. It is also certain that in the troubled years of the late fourth century and early third century BC posthumous issues were regularly made by the successors of Alexander, both of Alexander's (**232-3**) coinage and of Philip's. Both coinages had by that time attained a reputation as good money and were widely acceptable, even to the point of being imitated by Celtic tribes to the north of Greece. Once the coinage had become established, such continued desirability is understandable. It is far more difficult to see why Alexander may have had need to use coinage in the name of Philip and particularly gold staters which, if Le Rider's arrangement proves accurate, can hardly have gained a great reputation in a decade of use.

The invasion of Asia Minor

The assassination of Philip occurred after he had already begun an invasion of Asia Minor to liberate Greek cities from the Persian Empire. A Greek army under the Macedonian leader Parmenion was already in the field in Asia Minor, and in cities such as Ephesus revolution was already underway to welcome the liberators. The final issues in silver display evidence of a large and hurried coinage that must have been intended to finance this expedition. While heavy striking of Philip's coinage was taking place (**191**), with a number of different varieties closely interlinked by obverse dies – a sign of exceptional mint activity – the coinage of Alexander began, with new designs and with the silver on a new, heavier weight standard, but with the same group of symbols (**192**) that formed the last issues of his father's coinage. The reform of the Macedonian coinage that was one of Alexander's first acts as king took place in the middle of the feverish mint activity that was to provide coinage for the expedition into Asia.

The head of Heracles on the silver coinage was continued from the fractional coinage of Philip II and underlined the ancestral line of the Argead dynasty. The seated figure of Zeus was an innovation, but suited to the leadership of the Greek states claimed by both Philip and Alexander through their position as general of the Hellenic League. The types of the gold staters (**199**) were completely new to the coinage of the Macedonian kings. Athena may recall the city of Corinth on which was centred the Hellenic League. Victory, and particularly victory at sea signified by the mast held by the figure, would seem to look back to 480 BC when the Greeks 'united' to defeat the Persian fleet in the bay of Salamis.

There is no need to postulate a posthumous coinage of Philip II in silver until after the death of Philip III, but it does seem as if many gold issues in the name of Philip belong to the reign of Alexander. It must be assumed that they had to be struck because payment of some kind was demanded in this particular coinage. Since we know that Philip died leaving an empty treasury and five hundred talents of debts, such gold coins may have been required to meet these particular outstanding payments. Despite his own military expenses, Alexander had reduced his debts within two years to two hundred talents (still some fifty thousand gold staters at a ratio of silver to gold of 12:1).

Alexander's preparations for expeditions north into Thrace, south to Thebes and finally in 334 BC, across the Dardanelles onto Persian territory resulted in a large coinage from the Macedonian mints, and a third mint was added to the two established by Philip. It is notable that Alexander did not at once press on with the campaign started by his father, and it is very probable that the expeditions in Thrace and Greece, which politically established Alexander's position at home, were also intended to provide booty to help with the economic position. Ten years previously Timoleon had managed to stave off a desperate shortage of funds by selling the spoils of his campaign against the Carthaginians.

Alexander completed the domination of Greece and at the head of a force comprised of the member states of the League of Corinth he marched into Asia in 334 BC. His successes brought him to Tarsus and Phoenicia in 333, Egypt in 332, Babylon in 331, Bactria in 329 and India in 327 BC. It is important to remember that almost the whole of this area, despite its cultural diversity, had been under one adminstration for two hundred years, and wisely Alexander retained and adapted the systems of government that he found. The tribute previously payable to the Great King of Persia became payable to Alexander as King of Asia, and the vast wealth captured at the centres of Persian administration had to be turned to use to equip and reinforce the Greek army. Mints were set up to coin the imperial Macedonian issues at satrapal centres where tribute was collected and at strategic points on the crucial line of communications back to Macedonia. The earliest mint of the Alexander coinage on Asian soil was without doubt that at Tarsus. Some even believe that it was here that the imperial coinage was devised, long after the expedition had set out from Macedonia, with its new Attic weight 20 per cent heavier than the coinage of Philip, and with the reverse seated Zeus that was very similar in some respects to the Baal of Tarsus, whose figure had appeared on the Achaemenid coinage of Tarsus (195) and other Cilician cities in the years preceding the arrival of Alexander. The idea that Alexander delayed issuing his own coinage for three years, at a time when he had an army continuously in the field, is hardly plausible, and such similarities as have been seen between the Baal of Tarsus and the Zeus of Alexander's coinage are not more than the coincidence of engraving a similarly seated figure. It is, however, undoubtedly clear that at Tarsus the style of the cutting of many details shows that the same engravers, who had worked at the mint under the Achaemenid administration, turned their hands to create the dies for the new Alexander coinage (**196**).

Close attention to the style of the different engravers proves that one engraver was later taken from Tarsus to Ake (Acre) (**197**), a strategic point on the Phoenician coast, where an important mint was established to provide Alexander's imperial coinage. The style of engraving by this hand is found first in the sequence of issues located at Tarsus, and then it appears in the sequence placed at Ake. There is, furthermore, evidence of an actual obverse die transferring to Ake, having first been used in the sequence that may be attributed to Sidon. The linking of different series by a common obverse die is well attested elsewhere, in the Carthaginian coinage struck in Sicily, in the royal coinage of Lysimachus, in Cyprus under the domination of the Ptolemaic kings and in the Achaean League. Here it is clear that the setting up of a new mint at Ake entailed the drafting of engravers from elsewhere, and in this particular case a die presumably moved with its engraver to the new mint.

Other mints were soon established in Damascus and Aradus, and by 325 BC most areas of the empire bordering the Mediterranean had mints which provided a supply of Alexander's imperial coinage, although in Greece during his lifetime it was only in Macedonia that such issues were made.

Alexander brought the regular use of coinage – as opposed to the use or imitation of coin imported as bullion – to the whole of the Near East. In the generation before his arrival in Egypt in 332 BC, the Persian satraps had moved in this direction with their issues of imitations of the owl tetradrachms and drachmae of Athens, struck at Memphis (*see* chapter 5), and an issue recently identified from its Aramaic legend to have come from Syene (Aswan) (**163**). The last Persian satrap of Egypt, Mazaces, struck issues of silver and bronze signed with his own name. Alexander appears to have followed his example. A small bronze coin with the forepart of a Pegasus and the letter A on the reverse (**194**) has recently been identified as having been struck at Memphis. The obverse bears a helmeted head that is unquestionably the portrait of Alexander himself and the issue was very probably made at the time of Alexander's visit in 332 BC. Its purpose must have been to remove from circulation the bronze coins of his Achaemenid predecessor.

A mint was opened at Babylon soon after Alexander's arrival in October 331 BC. As King of Asia, Alexander had no more need to use coin in the East than did the Persian kings, but he must have been aware of the advantages of coinage in bringing order and uniformity to his administration. Although we are not told what part he himself played in the organization of the coinage for his empire, there are several indications behind the policies that suggest his complicity. We know that Philip II used his coinage to reflect his victory in the Olympic games, and the monetary reform that took place immediately after Alexander's accession is so dramatic and in such disregard for tradition that it is certainly possible that the king himself was responsible.

Along with the coins of Alexander's imperial designs on the Attic standard at key administrative points, it is important to emphasize that in several areas Alexander's governors struck local coinage on local weight standards. In Macedonia there is a series of issues with eagle reverse (**193**). The fractions of drachma and below can be firmly linked through the symbols with the main output of imperial tetradrachms, providing small denominations down to an obol. There are also staters on the local weight used by Philip, also with eagle reverse, which may have emanated from the ancient capital of the Argead dynasty, Aegae. The accompanying symbol is apparently a Persian headgear, with ties under the chin, a symbol which cannot be paralleled on any other issue. The significance is uncertain, but the coins may certainly be attributed to Macedonia, and not to any part of the Persian Empire.

In Cilicia, the god Baal of Tarsus who had appeared regularly on the Achaemenid coinage of the area, continued to be used on the reverse of silver staters struck by Alexander's governor, Balakros, also continuing the local weight standard. The obverse, however, a dramatic facing head of Athena in triple-crested helmet, is the same goddess who adorns Alexander's gold staters, a mixing of Greek and local images. One issue is signed by Balakros himself, presumably just before he died in 328 BC.

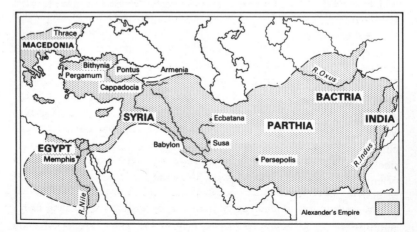

Fig. 10   *Alexander's Empire and the Hellenistic Kingdoms.*

From the sanctuary town of Hierapolis-Bambyce in Syria there is an even more poignant meeting of the cultures. The coins depict a lion on one side, and a horseman, no doubt Alexander himself, as on the five shekels from the east of his empire. The inscription is in Aramaic, but it is a clear transliteration of the name of Alexander (**198**). The lion appears again in Babylonia, where the Persian Mazaeus, Alexander's governor of the region from 331 to 328 BC, instituted a coinage known from the reverse as 'lion staters' (**217**). These show Baal on the other side. Mazaeus himself signed the early issues, and later the symbols and letters in many cases run parallel with the imperial coinage of the region. At least two mints produced this coinage, but the weights are very varied, occasionally reaching full Attic weight, but normally significantly below. It may be assumed that the standard was in reality the local Babylonian shekel, so that the coins become two shekel pieces. Their issue continued after Alexander's death, until his general Seleucus took the royal title in 305 BC.

Alexander's eastern empire

Alexander's imperial coinage was accepted everywhere. It is, however, absolutely clear from the numismatic record that Alexander adopted when convenient the minting practices of his Achaemenid predecessors and, like them, he saw no virtue in stamping out local coinage in order to replace it with his imperial Macedonian issues. Indeed, new coinage was created specifically for local circulation. We even find that in Mesopotamia he adopted the gold daric which, under the Persians, had been struck in Asia Minor only, and instituted double darics, one issue of which was signed by Stamenes the successor of Mazaeus as governor of Babylonia (**202**). Unashamedly Achaemenid coinage was struck by the conquering Macedonian!

The most dramatic of the coinages of this period, and of all Greek coinages, displays similar contradictions. Impressive silver 'medallions' of ten drachmae or, more probably, five shekels, were struck in the east of the empire (**200**). Their exact origin is not yet known. These show Alexander himself in cavalry uniform crowned by a flying figure of Victory, and holding the thunderbolt of Zeus as a reminder of the story current in his lifetime that he was actually the son of Zeus. On the other side is a scene of Alexander on his horse Bucephalus driving back an oriental potentate on his elephant. This must have been struck in 326 BC or shortly thereafter, and until recently only three had survived. A hoard in 1973 astounded the numismatic world by producing at least four more and, in addition, examples of a previously unknown tetradrachm or two shekel which, with the same letter and monogram, was clearly of the same issue (**201**). In contrast to the victory message of the 'medallion', the designs of the new denomination boast an Indian infantry bowman and a war elephant, the weapons of an oriental war machine. Together, the two coin types create a remarkable assertion of Alexander's policy of integrating what was good from the old régime with the new Macedonian system of rule. This coinage and the double darics of Mesopotamia provide an indisputable illustration of the policy which led to many criticisms among the Greeks that Alexander was becoming a barbarian oriental himself. Alexander wanted to foster in the whole of his empire a spirit of concord and community, despite the historical divisions of the various cultures that it embraced, and the coinage with its mixture of local and imperial elements plays its part in this.

The title of king appears on Alexander's coinage only towards the end of his life, and coincides with an upsurge of issues in the Near East. At the mint attributed to Babylon, the imperial coinage grew from fairly small beginnings to one of the largest outputs known from any mint in his reign. Each issue is marked with a symbol in addition to more permanent letter and monogram, and there is exceptionally close interlinking between the obverse dies of all issues. This may be interpreted to suggest that several issues were under production with different symbols at the same time. At the time when the royal title appears, there are fifteen different symbols that are found first without and then with the title (**203–4**). It is not impossible to envisage a very heavy coinage with fifteen sources of output. This group of issues occurs at the time when Alexander despatched back to Greece from Susa ten thousand of his troops, each with a talent (six thousand drachmae) as a reward for service. It seems very likely that the massive Mesopotamian issue could have been connected with this pay-off, and this may explain why these issues are found so widely dispersed over the whole of the empire and beyond. However, the sum involves fifteen million tetradrachms, and there is no possibility that the Babylonian mint could have produced such a quantity of coin from the seventy seven known tetradrachm obverse dies of this group. Other mints show a similar increase in activity towards the end of Alexander's life, and no doubt the money to complete the payment when the troops arrived in Greece was amassed from various sources. The seventy seven dies might have been sufficient for some fifteen hundred talents, and the decadrachms and gold staters that emanated at the same time would have supplemented that significantly.

Italy

Alexander died suddenly on 13 June 323 BC at the point, it is rumoured, of turning his attention to the west of the Mediterranean. The Carthaginians had been driven from the Greek colonies in Sicily by the dramatic expedition of Timoleon in 344 BC, and the spirit of the new freedom is emphasized by the large issue at Syracuse of bronze coins depicting the head of Zeus and labelled 'Zeus the bringer of freedom' (205). At the same time many small cities in Sicily used the earlier bronze coins of Syracuse on which to strike their own autonomous coinage (208), and for some this was the only period of coinage in the history of the city.

Italy had not suffered the Carthaginian invasion but, as mentioned in chapter 5, was far from free from internal disturbances. In 344 BC Tarentum, threatened by the indigenous peoples around her, called on Sparta, her mother city, for military support, in the same way that Syracuse turned to Corinth. Again in 334 BC Alexander of Epirus, who had succeeded in uniting that area as one kingdom, was invited to help Tarentum. Alexander's coinage in silver and gold struck in Italy reflects the Zeus and thunderbolt designs of Syracuse with their message of bringing freedom to the Greek colonies (206). Tarentum itself continued a major output of silver staters and fractions into the third century, and in about 320 BC a remarkable stater in gold was issued, depicting the young founder of the colony Taras with Poseidon (207). The exact occasion of issue is not known, but it was at a time of crisis at which the city was again appealing for help, as was the gold issue at Metapontum, struck at the time of the expedition of Alexander of Epirus. At the same time the silver coinage of Metapontum celebrates the hero Leukippos (209), the legendary founder of the city, with exceptional double staters joining the regular issues of staters. Here again it is the defence of the city that called for the issue, and the head of Victory on one issue, labelled with her name in Greek, underlines the military nature of the issues. The earliest silver coinage of Rome belongs to the end of the fourth century BC and fits into the general pattern of the coinage of the Italian region, where large issues from Etruria, Neapolis, Thurii and Velia supplied the needs of the states, mainly in the form of didrachms. These hardly circulated, and it may be assumed that in addition to providing a coinage for general purposes, military and otherwise, the coins were probably producing a profit for the state that ensured that the valuable silver was not re-exported.

Carthage and Syracuse

The coinage of Carthage in the fourth century BC consisted of gold staters, silver tetradrachms and bronze coins. The weight of the gold appears to have been chosen to enable the stater to pass for twenty five silver drachmae on the Attic standard. In about 320 BC the gold was alloyed with silver, and thereafter the staters are mainly of electrum, and the weight was reduced, probably to provide a ratio of fifteen silver drachmae to the stater. The issues in silver struck in Sicily eloquently record their military nature, with inscriptions in Punic script MHNT ('camp') (*cf.* **88**) or 'MMHNT ('people of the camp') probably minted at the Carthaginian base at Lilybaeum. Other tetradrachm issues emanated from Panormus (the Punic SYS) (**210**), Motya and other strongholds.

The coinage of the Sicilian Greeks never resumed the glory of the fifth century. The only precious metal coinage, apart from scattered fractional issues, after the expedition of Timoleon was from Syracuse, consisting mainly of Corinthian staters. The tyrant Agathocles came to power in 317 BC with his popular overthrow of the oligarchs, and appears to have been profoundly influenced by the success of Alexander the Great against the barbarian Persians. His first coinage continued the Corinthian designs, but added as the symbol his personal signature, a triskeles (**212**). He introduced gold drachmae (**213**) derived directly from the staters of Philip II with the head of Apollo and biga (**186**), but with the triskeles again prominently displayed, the chariot of course recalling the great fifth century coinage of Syracuse. He expanded his power over areas of eastern Sicily, but was prevented by the Carthaginians from capturing Acragas, and was himself blockaded in Syracuse in 311 BC. In the following year he introduced an important coinage of electrum (**214**), following Carthaginian precedent. He escaped through the blockade, and in alliance with Ophellas, governor of Cyrene for Ptolemy of Egypt and a former officer in Alexander's army, he was able to launch a dramatic expedition into Africa against Carthage herself. There can be little doubt that the inspiration for this bold move came from the success of the Macedonians whose coinage he copied.

The coinage of Cyrene under Ophellas had previously consisted of a fine series of gold staters and a remarkable array of small denominations. The silver coinage bore local designs with the silphium plant prominent (**211**), but Ophellas introduced the Attic standard, which was current at that time in Egypt. Aristotle (*Pollux* IX.62) is quoted as commenting that the gold denominations at Cyrene were the equivalent in silver of four tetradrachms, one tetradrachm and a didrachm, a silver/gold ratio of 15:1. This fell sharply to 10:1 under Ophellas, and then in line with Egypt began to rise again to 12:1. There was one issue of Alexander coinage at Cyrene, under Ophellas' successor, Magas, with the obverse head of Herakles unusually turned to the left.

At the time of the African expedition there was a revival at Syracuse of the tetradrachm of the fifth century type, but clearly marked with Agathocles' triskeles. The expedition crumbled as a result of the desert conditions, and Ophellas was murdered in 309 BC. Agathocles' return to Sicily was not without honour, and in about 305 BC he changed the designs of the tetradrachm to reflect his successes in Sicily and Africa with a reverse figure of Victory erecting a trophy, and signed with his name (**215**). In the early third century, gold issues appeared with the head of Athena derived from Alexander's staters and the thunderbolt of Zeus, and for the first time with his royal title which he had adopted in 304 BC.

The Diadochi

The development from a city to a regal coinage and the seemingly reluctant adoption of the royal title, which is clearly evident in Agathocles' coinage, is typical of its period. On the death of Alexander in Babylon on 13 June 323 BC, the agreement of his generals was to support his mentally retarded half-brother Philip III as king, making Perdiccas his regent in Greece. Two months later Alexander's son, Alexander IV, was born and he was made joint king. The coinage reflects these events. At Babylon, the years 323 to 322 BC saw a large output of coinage both of imperial types in gold (**216**) and silver and of lion staters (**218**), and the imperial issues are in the name of both Philip (**219**) and Alexander. Elsewhere we find a dovetailing of issues in the name of the two kings, so that the same variety is found in both names. In this way the 'posthumous' coinage of Alexander began, although in reality it was the coinage of his young son Alexander IV. In Macedonia only one issue of imperial tetradrachms was struck in the name of Philip III by the regent Perdiccas and his successors Antipater and Polyperchon. The silver and gold coinage of the types of Philip II provided such new currency as was required, together with imperial issues in the name of Alexander. It is clear that in Macedonia the spirit of Alexander still ruled, and the continuation of coinage in the name of Alexander, even after the death of Alexander IV in 316 BC, became the natural way to honour the memory of the dead leader. Cassander, son of Antipater and brother-in-law of Alexander, who had won the support of the Greek cities, came to power in Macedonia by driving out Polyperchon, and broke with tradition by introducing a new bronze coinage in his own name (**228**). His acceptance of the royal title in 306 BC is reflected in his later bronze issues, but he continued a silver coinage exclusively of posthumous tetradrachms in the name of Philip and of Alexander.

Despite the many factions that arose as the huge empire began to disintegrate, the coinage in the name of Alexander was a unifying element. Apart from the Macedonian coinage in the name of Philip, the only significant local issues to continue were the lion staters in Babylonia. The later varieties of these were signed by Seleucus with his anchor mark before his assumption of the royal title in 306 BC.

It is from such local coinage, however, that the regal coinages of the later kingdoms were born. Ptolemy was the first to introduce a new coinage (**220**), still in the name of Alexander and probably struck at the old capital, Memphis, rather than the new city of Alexandria. The portrait of the deified Alexander on the obverse depicts him wearing the scalp of an elephant. The parallel with Heracles in a lionskin is unmistakable, and the elephant must have recalled Alexander's victories over the Indians, as Heracles had triumphed over the Nemean lion. The elephant is also a symbol of eternity and thus became connected with the idea of deification. On later gold staters of Ptolemy I the figure of Alexander holding a thunderbolt is found in a chariot drawn by four elephants, as we know him to have been portrayed in a procession staged by Ptolemy II in the 270s in Alexandria. Alexander is shown wearing the elephant headdress on bronzes throughout the Ptolemaic period, and on silver this image was used until the introduction of Ptolemy's own portrait. A further detail in the design is the presence of the ram's horn of Zeus Ammon which can be seen in Alexander's hair. This is a reference to the claim that Alexander was the son of Zeus, first voiced during his visit to the oracle of Zeus Ammon at Siwa in Libya.

Soon after 315 BC, Ptolemy introduced a new reverse design, still retaining the portrait and name of Alexander but abandoning the Zeus of the Alexander imperial coinage. The new reverse shows the figure of Athena Alkidemos, the patron goddess of Pella in Macedonia, a significant reminder of Ptolemy's Macedonian origins. Within the short period of this series two interesting pieces suggest that changes took place in minting practices, and they introduce the name of Ptolemy to the coinage. The first is inscribed KYPANAION , which indicates the coin to be the product of the mint of Cyrene, at about the time of Ophellas' expedition against Carthage, and is the first overtly Ptolemaic coinage for the Cyrenaica. The other issue is inscribed AΛEΞANΔPEION which must be reference to the mint at Alexandria. It is possible that it was only at this time that the old mint at Memphis was replaced by one in the new capital of the satrapy. In about 310 BC this new coinage, which had continued the Attic weight of the previous issue, was reduced in weight by a diobol. The tetradrachm (**221**) of this reduced weight was about 15.7 grammes, and this reform coincides with a spate of countermarking of the earlier Attic weight tetradrachms of imperial type, most of which had entered Egypt from other parts of the empire. Hoards show that the countermarked heavier coins and the lighter coins were circulating together, and without doubt the lighter pieces were tariffed at the same purchasing power as the heavier pieces. The latter naturally disappeared from circulation fairly quickly, and this reform of the coinage effectively isolated the currency of Egypt from that of other areas of the former Macedonian Empire.

Towards the end of this coinage in the name of Alexander appear gold staters, also reduced to a weight which would allow five of the tetradrachms to pass for a stater (a silver/gold ratio of 11:1). These staters are clearly marked with the name and title of Ptolemy as king of Egypt. At about the same time bronze coins also began to be struck with Ptolemy's own name. The final step towards a truly Hellenistic coinage was taken in the later 290s with the introduction of the portrait of Ptolemy (**223**), who thus became one of the first of Alexander's successors to place his own image on coins. The weight of the tetradrachm was again reduced, this time by an obol or just over 4 per cent, and new denominations appear in bronze and gold (**222**). Soon afterwards, in about 290 BC, the weight of the tetradrachm fell yet again to stabilize at around 14.3 grammes, a reduction from the original weight of Alexander's coinage of about 17 per cent. The reason for this clearly lies in a rise in the value of gold against silver, since the final weights display a ratio of 12:1 (fifteen silver tetradrachms = 1 gold pentadrachm, or trichryson as it was called in papyri). Following this series of monetary reforms over twenty five years, which must have been extremely frustrating for the business community of Egypt, the system remained for a generation or so.

Elsewhere in the empire the last years of the fourth century BC saw the struggle of Antigonus the One-eyed to reunite the empire of Alexander under his leadership. On the death of Antipater in 319 BC, Antigonus became general of the army in Asia Minor and came to wield power through his military superiority. This caused a counter alliance of the generals Cassander of Macedonia, Ptolemy of Egypt, Lysimachus of Thrace and Seleucus of Syria. At the battle of Ipsus in 301 BC Antigonus was defeated and killed. Although he had adopted the title of king, the only royal coinage issued in the area under his authority was that in the name of Alexander. His influence was felt at Ake, where the date of his arrival in 315 BC becomes the base date for an era which appears on the last issues of the Alexander coinage at that mint, in the years 307 to 304 BC.

Antigonus had forced Seleucus to leave Mesopotamia and take refuge with Ptolemy in Egypt, and the date of the triumphant return of Seleucus to Babylon on 7 October 312 BC was seen to be a moment of great importance, signifying as it did the beginning of the kingdom of Syria and the foundation of the Seleucid dynasty. It became the base for the 'Seleucid' era widely used in areas belonging to the kingdom of Syria and surviving, as the era of Antioch, through Christian times to the fifteenth century. The presence of Seleucus is first felt in the Mesopotamian region when his seal, the anchor, was introduced onto the lion staters as an unchanging symbol of authority (**224**). The same mark is to be found on the contemporary imperial coinage in the name of Alexander at mints at Susa, Ecbatana in Media, and on the Pheonician coast. Seleucus took the title of king in 306 BC, and in the following year coinage bearing his own name was produced at Susa (225). It has traditionally been believed that the first coinage of Seleucus was of the Alexander types in silver and gold, but altered to include his own name and title. Recent research has shown, however, that the coinage of Alexander types signed with the name of Seleucus belongs to the final years of his reign, and is die-linked to the first issues of his son, Antiochus. The coinage that began in about 305 BC was of new designs, following the precedent set by Ptolemy, but the full Attic weight was retained.

The obverse for this new coinage shows a portrait head wearing a helmet covered in a panther skin and decorated with a bull's horn and ear. All these elements are to be identified with Dionysus, who was recognized in mythology to have conquered the East and who had even invaded India. The portrait is that of Alexander, deified and assimilated to Dionysus himself. The reverse figure of Victory erecting a trophy repeats the theme of the conquest of the East. Quite apart from Seleucus using Alexander as the tutelary deity of his kingdom, there is a more particular reference to be recognized in the designs, to Seleucus' own success in campaigns on his eastern border and the final peace with the Indian King Chandragupta at about the time of the issue of this series. The special nature of this brief coinage is emphasized by there being parallel issues, with the same issue marks, of the normal imperial coinage in the name of Alexander. A number of silver-plated tetradrachms are known of this 'victory' coinage at Susa, which are believed to have emanated from the mint itself and not to be contemporary imitations. It may have been lack of public confidence due to such plated pieces that shortly afterwards led to a dramatic change in the designs.

Again, the Attic standard was retained, but the new coinage (226) was struck at several places including the new capital of Seleuceia on the Tigris (Baghdad), Susa, Ecbatana and Bactra in the far East. The head of Zeus on the obverse of this coinage shows strong Macedonian influence, but the chariot drawn by elephants on the reverse is a completely oriental feature. It is reminiscent of Ptolemy's gold coinage of the same period, but the driver of the chariot is Athena armed for war, not Alexander, a dramatic design owing nothing to Seleucus' predecessor. The elephant is also used on the reverse of a series of bronze coins (227), a reminder, perhaps, that Chandragupta had given Seleucus five hundred war elephants.

Demetrius Poliorcetes

To the West the son of Antigonus, Demetrius, nicknamed the Besieger (Poliorcetes), actively continued his father's campaign to be heralded as the true successor of Alexander. He gained notable successes. In 306 BC he defeated Ptolemy in a sea battle off Salamis, Cyprus, during his siege of the city, and he was awarded the royal title by his father. He followed this by invading Greece, and took from Cassander control of key Greek cities such as Corinth and ultimately attained the throne of Macedonia for a short period, from 294 to 288 BC. Unlike his father, Demetrius displayed his name and title on his coinage, after a period in which he issued the imperial gold and silver coinage in the name of Alexander.

Not long after his acceptance of the royal title, Demetrius introduced a coinage of silver tetradrachms (**229**) and a few smaller fractions which celebrate his great victory at Salamis. On one side a figure of Victory stands on the prow of a galley blowing a trumpet. On the other stands the sea god, Poseidon, hurling his trident on behalf of Demetrius. The later coinage of Demetrius (**230**) depicts the portrait of the king clearly imitating the posthumous portraits of Alexander wearing the horn of Ammon. Demetrius is shown with a prominent bull's horn emerging from his forehead. The bull was sacred to Poseidon, and so the horn provides a clear reference to Demetrius' claim to be a son of Poseidon. He also wears a ribbon diadem as a mark of kingship. On the reverse, Poseidon is shown either seated, like the Zeus Nikephoros of Alexander but holding an aplustre, a trophy seized from a captured galley, or standing, foot on rock, watching intently over the successes of his 'son' Demetrius. A rare coinage of gold staters also uses his portrait on the obverse, and on the reverse a horseman charging into battle with lowered sarissa, a variant on the traditional horseman theme of Macedonian coinage, and reminiscent of the figure of Alexander and Bucephalus on the silver five shekel (**200**) celebrating Alexander's victories in India.

In contrast to his coinage in precious metals, Demetrius rarely placed his name on his bronze coinages (**231**) which normally bear an abbreviation of the royal title and sometimes the monogram of his name. His portrait has been seen in the head with Corinthian helmet on an anonymous bronze series with prow reverse, but the identification is far from certain and most people handling the coin in ancient and in modern times would identify the head as Athena's. It is interesting that it was clearly felt that the royal portrait was unsuitable for bronze coinage, for this phenomenon is evident in the coinage of all the diadochi.

Although he was a most able general, Demetrius' ambitions brought him into conflict with the other diadochi and in 288 BC Seleucus and

Ptolemy united with his neighbour, Lysimachus of Thrace, against him, and the people of Macedonia itself deserted him. His attempts to conquer Lysimachus in Thrace and Asia Minor failed, and he ultimately surrendered to Seleucus in 285 BC and died in captivity two years later.

Lysimachus

Lysimachus was allotted the area of Thrace and the Black Sea in the division of Alexander's empire. This area apparently had no imperial mint under Alexander, although Lysimachus may have had access to the mint at Amphipolis. He too took the title of King in 306/5 BC, and on the death of Cassander began to issue his new coinage, mainly of tetradrachms, at mints under his control in Thrace, Macedonia and Asia Minor, where he had come to power as a result of the defeat of Antigonus at Ipsus in 301 BC. After a brief coinage of Alexander type (**233**), Lysimachus introduced on his precious metal coinage a very fine portrait of Alexander wearing the ram's horn prominently in his hair (**234**). On the reverse he placed the seated figure of Athena, which was to become the prototype for the figures of Roma and Britannia. In the inevitable struggle with Seleucus, Lysimachus was defeated and killed at Corupedium in Lydia, but his coinage had become established in the Black Sea region and continued to be minted after his death.

Other diadochi

Numerous other generals figure in the period of unrest that followed the break-up of Alexander's kingdom. Many, such as Pleistarchos in Cilicia, did not strike coins in their own name, but their activities are mirrored in the large issues of posthumous Alexander coinage from mints under their control.

Pyrrhus of Epirus must similarly have used such coinage in his efforts to attain the Macedonian throne. There are plenty of bronze issues that can be attributed to him, presumably struck at his capital at Ambracia, but his fine gold and silver coinage all appears to belong to the period when he was fighting in Italy and Sicily on behalf of Tarentum against Rome and the Carthaginians. These issues were struck at Italian mints (**235**). He claimed descent from Achilles and Thetis, and it is they who feature on his coinage and illustrate his claim that he, as a descendent of the Greek hero, was going to wage a new Trojan war on the descendents of Aeneas.

The cities under Macedonian control in Greece and Asia Minor continued to strike coinage for use locally, but their precious metal issues were much reduced, presumably because such silver as was available was transferred to the coffers of the diadochi. The massive issues of staters of Corinth, for example, dwindle to a halt, and during the period of occupation by Demetrius there were issues of imperial Alexander coinage. One of the last issues of Corinth can be linked with the brief occupation of the area of Ptolemy, (308–306 BC). At Athens, Lachares, a friend of Cassander, seized power in 300 BC and used gold from the cult statue of Athena to pay his troops (**236**). These gold staters are clearly identifiable but, because of their stylistic similarity to the tetradrachms, they clearly mark the end of activity at the Athenian mint. There are few silver issues which can be placed between the time of Lachares and the second century.

King Areus (309/8–265 BC) was the first to produce coinage for the people of Sparta and this also appears to have been created at a time of military preparations. There are several issues in the name of Alexander from Peloponnesian mints, but none can be certainly attributed to Sparta. At the time of the outbreak of the Chremonidean War in 267 BC, when the Athenians, Peloponnesians and Ptolemy II united in an attempt to break the power of Macedonia, there is an issue of tetradrachms of Alexander's imperial types but in the name of Areus. The king died in battle at Corinth in 265 BC. By this time Alexander had been dead nearly sixty years, and the pattern of kingdoms that had emerged was to have a profound effect on the political history for centuries to come. The coinage traces the development of the move of the diadochi from being generals of Alexander to kings in their own right.

CHAPTER 8

The Hellenistic world

Coins reflect in some detail the political history of the last three centuries BC. As a result of the creation of the Macedonian Empire in the East and of the Carthaginian Empire in the West, the use of coinage as an everyday monetary medium had become widespread throughout the Greek-speaking world and beyond. The fourth century had witnessed the establishment of bronze coinage, and in the later part of the century there was a great increase in the number of cities that began to mint their own coins in bronze and small denomination silver. This development continued into the Hellenistic period so that, beside the coinages of the great monarchies and of the states which had adopted the issue of a regular coinage earlier, there are to be found the numerous sporadic issues from small cities, some unknown apart from their coins. Smaller kingdoms sought autonomy and broke away from the great monarchies, as Pontus, Bithynia, Pergamum, Armenia, Judaea, Nabathaea, Parthia, Bactria and others arose from within the Seleucid kingdom and each began to mint new coinages. The importance of the bronze coinage to a small state is illustrated in an inscription honouring Menas at the city of Sestos on the north shore of the Dardanelles (*OGIS* 339). One of his benefactions to the city was to pay for the production of the city's bronze coinage, which was seen to boost its self-esteem as well as to provide a fair profit to the treasury. With these bronze coinages added to precious metal issues the variety and complexity of Hellenistic coinage becomes almost bewildering, and no coherent account of it has ever been produced. The following sections look briefly at some of the fascinating developments of coinage in this period.

Portraiture

The generation that followed Alexander's death saw the general acceptance of the idea that the portrait of the reigning monarch was a suitable subject for a coin design. This had its roots in the use of portraiture on coins in the late fifth and fourth century BC by the Persian satraps and their vassals in Lycia (**157**). The worship accorded the monarch in the eastern world may certainly have influenced the use of the portrait as a coin type, for it could be seen to differ only slightly from the use of depictions of other deities. The period of hesitation when the head of the deified Alexander slowly gave way to that of the reigning monarch underlines the reticence with which such eastern practices could be accepted amongst the Greeks. The rulers of the Hellenistic period have left a great gallery of faces in their coinage that can be matched in no other medium, and it is due directly to the influence that these portraits later had on the Roman emperors that we find it so normal today to place the monarch's image on coins of the realm. There are two exciting elements in Hellenistic portraits that raise them above those of any other single period. First, although the die engraving tends not to be as deep-cut as in the fourth century and earlier, and there is a general movement towards flatter, less chunky coins, the designs still display sufficient relief to make the portrait stand out as a finely modelled representation of the particular head. There may be idealization in the way that the features are portrayed, but each head is nevertheless clearly distinct.

Secondly there is a tremendous variety in these portraits. The different cultural origins of those portrayed are often visible in their faces, but it is in the headgear particularly that they are differentiated. The diadochi evolved the simple ribbon diadem as the mark of kingship, and this continued to be used amongst the Greek monarchies. The portrayal of the queens begins with Philistis at Syracuse (**238**). She too wears the diadem, but the back of her head is covered in a flowing veil, and this becomes the accepted way to depict the queen until the time of Cleopatra VII of Egypt. The portraits of the king and queen, two deities side by side ('jugate') was introduced as a coin design by Ptolemy II (**290**), who placed his parents Ptolemy I and Berenice, clearly labelled gods ($\Theta E \Omega N$) on one side, and himself and his sister-queen, Arsinoe II, who was deified on her death in 270 BC, on the other. The Syrian kingdom continued this method of depicting two persons on one side of the coin. Laodice (**271**), wife of Antiochus III, is shown with her five-year-old grandson, Antiochus, son of Seleucus IV, for whom she was regent for a short time in 175 BC, before the boy was murdered by his uncle, Antiochus IV. The remarkable Cleopatra Thea, daughter of Ptolemy VI, who married in succession King Alexander Balas (150-146 BC), Demetrius II (146-140 BC) and Antiochus VII (139-129 BC), is found side by side with her first husband, and again with her son Antiochus VIII during their joint reign, (125-121 BC) (**276**).

In the smaller eastern kingdoms, the crown of each is clearly displayed on the monarch's head. In Persis (289) this takes the form of a cap that is clearly derived from that of the Persian satraps of the fourth century BC. In Armenia (277) and Commagene the highly decorated tiaras are surmounted by pointed crenellations, like mediaeval crowns, symbolizing the sun's rays.

Bactria, India, and Parthia

In the far east the kingdom of Bactria illustrates the continuation of Greek traditions far from the centres of Greek culture. There appears to have been a continuation of Alexander's policy of integrating the population, and this results in the gradual but persistent influence of Indian culture, clearly visible on the coinage. The coins themselves form a major source of information on the history of the area, and much has to be gleaned from the study of the designs, issue marks and inscriptions, and from the patterns of circulation recorded by finds made in modern times. The kingdom was founded by Diodotus, governor of the area under Antiochus I and II of Syria, whose absolute power, in the manner of the earlier Persian satraps, enabled him first to place his own portrait on the coins, wearing the diadem of kingship but retaining the inscription in the name of Antiochus II (279). Only later did Diodotus coin in his own name (280). The foundation of this particular kingdom was made with the full compliance of the Syrian monarch who saw it as a buffer with the Indian Empire beyond. Indeed, Antiochus forged an alliance with Diodotus by giving him his sister in marriage.

The death of Diodotus in about 235 BC was followed by an expedition by Antiochus III in an attempt to reconquer the whole of Alexander's former eastern empire. In Bactria he was met by Euthydemus, a Greek from Magnesia who had married the daughter of Diodotus and taken the throne. The resulting treaty settled the future of the new kingdom. Euthydemus' son, Demetrius (c.200-185 BC) appears to have carried out the conquest of which Antiochus had dreamed, in reconquering the Indian territories of Alexander's empire which had been taken by Chandragupta at the end of the fourth century. The coins show Demetrius wearing the elephant scalp headdress, as conqueror of India and in direct imitation of the portrait of Alexander.

The sequence of kings at this time becomes confused, and the exact areas governed by each is still not known. Antimachus (281) depicts himself wearing a hat of a different sort, the Macedonian horseman's flat kausia, a clear statement of the ruler's origins. At about the same time King Agathocles struck a remarkable series of tetradrachms with dynastic portraits. Alexander, wearing the lionskin headdress of

Herakles, is clearly labelled Alexander, son of Philip (**284**). This group of issues also includes portraits of Diodotus, Euthydemus, Pantaleon, Antiochus III and Demetrius depicted in his elephant scalp headress. At the same time local bronze coins were struck, square in shape, as was so popular in India (**286**), with designs of deities taken from the Indian pantheon and with reverse inscriptions in the Brahmi script. This transcription of the Indian prakrit language is known from the time of Asoka, the successor of Chandragupta, and is first found on the coins of Pantaleon. It reads from left to right, whereas Kharosthi, a script also transliterating prakrit but dating from Achaemenid times, reads from right to left. This was introduced onto coins by Antimachus and Eucratides. Here and elsewhere it is important to note the different origins of the designs of the bronze coinages and the tetradrachms. The former were, of course, designed to appeal to the mass of the population, while the tetradrachms would have been mainly used by the ruling classes.

In Bactria itself Eucratides seized power in about 170 BC, ruling mainly in the northern area. His magnificent coinage belies a reign of military activity. In addition to large issues of tetradrachms, there was one issue of gigantic gold coins of twenty staters, over 168 grammes (**282**), the largest of all Greek coins. He too adopted the 'jugate' portrait to depict on his coins the images of Heliocles and Laodice (**283**), believed by many to be his parents. It is interesting that Heliocles wears no attribute of kingship, possibly because he was neither of royal blood nor deified. Laodice is shown with a diadem, and it is believed that it was through her that Eucratides claimed the throne. Eucratides himself wears a distinctive helmet that is decorated with a bull's horn and ear, the same symbols found on the portrait of Alexander on the victory coinage of Seleucus I. This form of helmet was adopted by his successors in India as a mark of kingship.

Eucratides' son, Heliocles, had probably ruled southern Bactria during his father's reign, but the whole of the Bactrian kingdom appears to have succumbed to invasion by the Sakas from the North after Eucratides' death, about 140 BC. The recently conquered territories in India, however, provided a continuation of the Greek ruling presence, with their capital at Taxila. From the time of Menander (*c*.165-130 BC) the inscription on the reverse of the coins regularly repeats the name and titles of the monarch in Kharosthi, although the designs themselves clearly derive from the Greek repertoire. A remarkable type of portrait, adopted from the mid-second century BC, shows the head and shoulders of the king, but with his arm raised in the act of hurling a spear. The military preoccupations of the rulers made this type of portrait popular in later years. An exceptional issue was the double decadrachm (84 grammes) in silver struck by Amyntas (c.100-75 BC). The king wears the helmet introduced by Eucratides, and on the reverse is a fine depiction of Zeus enthroned, and holding a figure of victory, a palm branch and his sceptre. This illustrates the final stages of Greek coinage in India. With only limited contact with the Mediterranean world the return to Indian culture was inevitable.

To the west of Bactria the kingdom of Parthia was founded in about 238 BC by Arsaces. Andragoras, who had established himself in the Seleucid satrapy in the area, was driven out. The only coinage that can be attributed to Arsaces consists of drachmae showing him wearing the leather cap of the Persian satraps (287). The area was regained by Antiochus III, but from the middle of the second century there were regular issues of drachmae, tetradrachms and bronze. The regular use of the same reverse designs and the general lack of variety make for a uniformity bordering on the monotonous. There are serious problems of chronology because, although each monarch bore a distinctive name and title, the coinage was issued under the dynastic name of Arsaces and the accompanying titles are not sufficiently explicit to allow certain identification with the monarchs known from other historical sources. However, Orodes II (c.57-38 BC) began to place on the tetradrachms the month of issue, using the Greek names and, later, the year reckoned on the Seleucid era based on October (Dios) 312 BC, so that thereafter the date of each isue can be pinpointed with remarkable accuracy (288).

Posthumous portraits

We have seen the idea of the posthumous portrait on coins used by the successors of Alexander to enhance their prestige. In the Greek monarchies of Egypt and Pergamum the ubiquitous use of the portrait of the founder of the dynasty makes for problems of chronology. Ptolemy I introduced his own portrait in the first decade of the third century BC, and until the end of the dynasty in 31 BC his portrait continued to provide the obverse for silver issues, with very few exceptions. Ptolemy III sent a subsidy of silver and bronze coins to the Achaean League in the Peloponnese in the 220s BC. Although this issue was probably struck in Alexandria, the coins which may be attributed to this gift are always found in Greece and never in Egypt. They differ from all his other coinage from Egypt in having his portrait on the obverse. He also introduced the convention, followed by Ptolemy IV and Ptolemy V in the last quarter of the third century, of using his own portrait for coinage struck at cities in his Phoenician possessions.

The dramatic gold *mnaieia* of the later third century (octadrachms worth a hundred Attic drachmae) normally feature the head either of the deified Arsinoe II, daughter of Ptolemy I and wife of her brother Ptolemy II (**296**), or of Berenice II, queen of Ptolemy III (**294**). The reverses of the gold issue of Berenice contain two stars, a reminder that a group of stars was named the Lock of Berenice in her honour by Conon, the court astronomer. The caps of Castor and Pollux, themselves connected with the constellation Gemini, are found on her silver coins. The queens are always shown wearing the royal diadem and veil, and Arsinoe is shown with a sceptre across her shoulder, the flowered tip of which appears at the top of her head. These issues in gold were struck both in the Phoenician possessions and in Alexandria, and the portrait of Berenice occurs on a long sequence of coins in silver and bronze struck at the city of Marathus, Phoenicia, and dated according to the local era. These issues began during her lifetime in 227/6 BC and continued down to 152/1 BC, showing how a city might do honour to a benefactor.

The kingdom of Pergamum was centred upon the stronghold used by Alexander, Lysimachus and Seleucus as the storehouse for great wealth. The general entrusted with this by Lysimachus was the eunuch Philetaerus, who opportunely deserted to Seleucus in 282 BC. He issued a tetradrachm coinage in his own name, but without adopting the royal title, and placed the portrait of Seleucus on the obverse. His nephew and successor, Eumenes (263-241 BC), continued the reverse design in the name of Philetaerus, but changed the portrait to that of his uncle. Thus the coinage continued with very little variation (**256**), and with no identification of the ruling king, until the Attic weight royal tetradrachms ceased to be struck, just before 175 BC.

Developments in silver coinage

The Attic standard for silver coinage was inherited by the Hellenistic kingdoms from Alexander the Great and, before that, from the Athenian tetradrachms that had circulated widely in the East. The general acceptance from Italy to India of the coinage in the name of Alexander led to such coins being struck down to the first century BC. There was a lull in their production in the mid-third century, but with renewed coining in the Peloponnese, Black Sea, Asia Minor and Phoenicia in about 225 BC, this truly international coinage set the pattern for the Attic standard until after 175 BC. At about this time, most of the posthumous Alexander coinages came to an end, but in the Black Sea area, on the Thracian coast, Mesembria and Odessus continued their production into the first century (**248**). The reason for the continuation there was undoubtedly to make payments to the chieftains of the interior to ensure the protection of the cities from invasion by Celtic or local Thracian tribes.

The first and, for a long time, the only Hellenistic monarch to abandon the Attic weight standard was Ptolemy, who reduced his precious metal currency to the standard of his Phoenician possessions, the Tyrian shekel, a depreciation of over a half drachma in the tetradrachm. However, it would appear that the purchasing power of the coins was retained at a much higher value than that of the metal in them, and so in this way Ptolemy created a coinage that was considerably overvalued and which tended to circulate only within the territory of his kingdom. Those entering Egypt were obliged to exchange their coin into the local royal coinage, which alone was allowed to circulate within the kingdom. An interesting papyrus of 258 BC shows the administrative chaos that could result from the imposition of strict currency regulations. Demetrius, the director of the mint at Alexandria, had to write to Apollonios the local governor at a time of recoinage of gold coins to say that neither the mint nor any of the bankers could accept any of the earlier gold coinage or foreign gold, since they did not know the exchange rate. The occasion for this recoinage must have been the introduction of the gold octadrachms (mnaieia) and tetradrachms with the portraits of Ptolemy I and II jugate with their queens (**290**). These were worth a hundred silver drachmae and fifty silver drachmae on the Attic standard respectively, and they were replacing the gold 'pentadrachms' (trichrysa) and tenths of Ptolemy I, worth sixty and six silver drachmae. The problem of the exchange between the old and new denominations is self-evident since, unless huge amounts were being changed, exchange could only be effected through the medium of silver. This was, of course, causing considerable inconvenience in commercial circles, but it required a royal edict to resolve such a matter.

The end of the Attic weight coinage of Pergamum depicting the portrait of Philetaerus came in about 175 BC, at a time of a similar reform. These coins were replaced by a coinage without the name of any king, but nonetheless a royal coinage for the kingdom. The issues were struck at several cities which were named on the reverse (**259**). The designs of the new coinage celebrated Dionysus (the cista mystica in wreath of ivy) and Heracles (bowcase and, on the fractions, club and lionskin), from whom the Attalid kings claimed descent, and the coins became universally known as cistophori, a name which became attached to the weight standard. The weight to which they were struck represented a reduction of 25 per cent in the silver content, a drachma in the tetradrachm, and since these coins too are rarely found outside the area of the kingdom, this must involve a similar overvaluation. At about the same time, at the beginning of the final war between Macedonia and Rome (172-168 BC), King Perseus made a similar, though less drastic reduction in the weight of his coinage, but without altering the designs.

PLATE 17   Diadochi: Macedonia, Thrace, Greece

228   229   230   231

232   233   234

236

235   237

PLATE 18   Hellenistic Macedonia, Athens, Byzantium

238

239

240

241

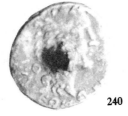

242

243

244

247

245

246

PLATE 19   Hellenistic Black Sea, Asia Minor

PLATE 20   Hellenistic Asia Minor, Near East

259

260

261

262

263

264

265

266

267

268

269

270

PLATE 21   Hellenistic Syria

271

272

273

274

275

276

277

278

PLATE 22   Hellenistic Bactria

279

280

281

282

283

284

PLATE 23　　Hellenistic India, Parthia, Persis, Egypt

285

286

287

288

289

290

291

292

293

PLATE 24   Hellenistic Egypt, Carthage

294   295

296   297

298   299

300   301   302

The tetradrachms fell by the weight of a diobol to just under 15.5 grammes. This reform was clearly instigated by the need to conserve stocks of silver in the face of the heavy military expenditure that the war would entail, and Perseus was rewarded with a reputation for being a miser.·

These reforms also coincide with a reduction in the weight of the silver coins of the Seleucid kings in Syria. This is so slight that it has only recently been realized that the reform took place at a particular time. The full Attic weight of the tetradrachms of Alexander was about 17.3 grammes. This fell gradually in the third century BC, but in the royal coinage at Antioch there was a fairly sudden drop to 16.8 grammes in about 172 BC. The weight fell again to 16.3 grammes at the end of the second century, and by the time of the final issues of the Seleucids in the second quarter of the first century under Philip and Tigranes, the weight of the tetradrachm was down to below 16 grammes.

There can be no doubt that the fall in weight of the silver coins must be related to a fall in the availability of silver and a consequent rise in its value. This is visible in the papyri of Egypt. Between 9 September 183 and 23 October 182 BC the price of silver doubled, the ratio to bronze leaping from 1:60 to 1:120. In 173 BC severe inflation raised the ratio to 1:480, at the very time when silver coinage elsewhere was undergoing reduction in weight. This was a time of tense political crisis, which in 170 BC led to the invasion of Egypt by Syria. To exacerbate the economic problems further, the Roman conquests in Spain, which ensured for Rome access to the important silver mines in that region, probably resulted in a cessation of any trade in silver that might previously have come to the eastern Mediterranean via Carthage. The important mines at Laurium in Attica were also worked on a considerably reduced scale in the Hellenistic period. The coinage of Athens itself was very small in the third century, but at the very time that the Seleucids and Macedonians were reducing the weights of their coins the Athenians began their large coinage known to the ancients, from the reverse design, as 'stephanephori', but in modern times called the New Style coinage (241-4). The obverse depicted the head of the cult image of Athena in the Parthenon. The reverse showed her owl standing on an amphora, with the whole design enclosed in an olive wreath. The major source of silver for this coinage does not appear to have been the mines at Laurium, most of which are believed to have lain idle throughout the Hellenistic period, and it is possible that the silver was channelled to Athens via the great emporium under her control at Delos and from other sources. Although this New Style coinage has the appearance of autonomous city issues, there is every reason to believe that the Romans adopted it as the official coinage of the province of Achaea. It stands out as the major coinage of the late Hellenistic period and the coins travelled extensively to North Greece, Asia Minor and Syria.

Countermarks

Unlike Egypt, the kingdoms of Pergamum and Syria did not bar the circulation of full Attic weight coinage. The late posthumous issues of Alexander tetradrachms, particularly those from the southern area of Asia Minor and the autonomous coinage of Side from the same region, travelled to Syria in large numbers, and at the time of the reform of Antiochus IV reducing the weight of the Syrian royal coinage, these foreign tetradrachms were countermarked for circulation with the official mark of the state, the Seleucid anchor (**268**). The value as currency of the two types of tetradrachm was clearly the same. There are other countermarks from the Syrian region permitting the circulation of foreign coin. One such is the personal mark, an unusual helmet, of the usurper Tryphon, uncle and regent of the young Antiochus VI, who murdered his charge and seized the throne in 142 BC. His coinage bears the titles king and emperor (autokrator), the first use on coins of the latter term which was to become so familiar under the Roman empire.

In the kingdom of Pergamum a similar phenomenon occurred at the time of the introduction of the cistophori. A countermark of a bowcase, clearly to be related to the reverse of the new lightweight coinage and accompanied by letters indicating the name of different cities, was applied to Attic weight coinage found to be circulating in the kingdom (**267**). Most of the cities identifiable on these countermarks are also known to have struck cistophori, and there is thus no doubt that the introduction of the new coinage was accompanied by countermarking existing stocks of coinage in a transition period. The countermark must also have equated the heavier and lighter coins as the same denomination for circulation.

A little earlier the same purpose can be detected at Byzantium and Calchedon, two cities having a history of monetary cooperation (*see* chapter 5). Both cities coined Attic weight issues in the third century BC of the types and in the name of Lysimachus, with one issue by Calchedon using the ethnic in place of the king's name. In about 230 BC both cities reformed their coinage, introducing autonomous issues on the lighter Phoenician standard, a brief interlude which came to an end with the resumption of posthumous Lysimachus issues in about 220 BC (**245**). At the time of the reform the existing coinage was called in and reissued with countermarks. The prow and letters Π Y for Byzantium (**246**), and the bust of Demeter or Apollo with the monogram of K A for Calchedon clearly indicate the official nature of these marks. That of Byzantium is even accompanied by a variable monogram which indicates the name of a person, and three of the six can be related to the names of the city magistrates, the hieromnemones, who signed the new reduced weight coinage.

The countermarks on bronze coins are also to be found at a time when there appears to have been a change in the size of the denominations. As with the silver coinages, the countermark is often to be related to restriking, and indeed the countermark is sometimes applied using both punch and anvil dies, perhaps as a pincer, so that the punch of the small countermark on the reverse also produces a small design in relief on the other side. This occurs in silver at Sinope (**255**), but is more common on bronze coins at places such as Erythrae and Panticapaeum (**253**). The design of the countermark on bronze coins can quite often be related to the design of a new coinage, frequently of a different size, so that as on silver the countermark equates for purposes of circulation coins of unequal appearance.

Experiments in coinage metals

Towards the end of the Hellenistic period in Egypt there is a marked drop in the fineness of the alloy of the tetradrachm. During the reign of Ptolemy XII (80-51 BC) there began a decline in the amount of silver in the tetradrachm, which falls from over 90 per cent to less than 50 per cent in the time of Cleopatra VII. Adulteration of the alloy obviously had the same effect as lowering the weight, as far as saving in silver was concerned, and in Egypt this paved the way for the billon tetradrachms of Alexandria that provided coinage for the Roman province.

Conscious adulteration of the alloy has been seen from the very earliest electrum coinage. The use of electrum continued into the Hellenistic period at Carthage, and there too the third century saw an extensive use of billon coinage, in which the silver in the coinage was dramatically reduced and the weight of the piece was made up by the addition of copper and lead.

It has recently been discovered that at the time of the Libyan revolt (241-238 BC) copper mixed with arsenic was used as a metal for coinage (**302**). The effect was to give a good silvery appearance to the finished product, and such improvement in its appearance was clearly thought to affect its acceptability. In about 174 BC in Bactria the kings Pantaleon, Agathocles (**285**) and Euthydemus II adopted a fashion for using natural copper-nickel for coinage, doubtless for the same reason, since the coin designs do not appear to differ from the ordinary copper pieces. In the early first century BC, during the reign of Mithradates VI, the cities of

Pontus (**250**) experimented with adding zinc to bronze coins, giving them an attractive gold appearance. This alloy, well-recognized as orichalcum, had a long history and was adopted by the Roman emperors for regular use as a coinage metal.

Bronze coinage

The increased use of bronze coinage in the Hellenistic period led to a number of experiments. The most dramatic was the transformation of the coinage in Egypt by Ptolemy II (285-246 BC), who was also responsible for the grand building schemes of the Museum, the Library and the Pharos at Alexandria. He produced bronze coins of such a size and weight that the public were clearly intended to be impressed by the quantity of metal in each piece. It would seem that the heaviest denomination of 96 grammes was the half drachma, since the next largest denomination at 72 grammes and with two eagles on the reverse becomes the diobol, if the smallest fraction (3 grammes) is made the chalkous or twelfth of an obol. Although not exactly the equivalent in bronze of their silver denominations, at the normal ratio of bronze to silver in Egyptian papyri of 60:1, the impression is given that these bronze denominations are good value and trustworthy pieces (**293**). Their introduction occurred about 260 BC after Ptolemy's attempt to gain a foothold in Greece and Macedonia. The coinage found in the Ptolemaic camp sites of the 260s at Koroni, in Attica, and elsewhere consisted of the issues that immediately preceded this reform of the bronze denominations (**291**). In the reign of Ptolemy III (246-221 BC) a further reform took place which apparently did make the coins the equivalent of their bullion value. The largest denomination weighed 105 grammes, the equivalent of one and a half obols in terms of silver. A little later, in about 225 BC, a third reform reduced the size of the coins to their previous denominations, but improved their appearance by using a metal with a fine yellowish hue. Thereafter there are several further reforms reducing the coins to small tokens, but after the middle of the second century there were no official bronze coins minted in Egypt until the time of Cleopatra VII in the 30s BC.

The coins of Cleopatra, in two denominations, are marked with the letters M and Π (**299**), which apparently refer to the value of the coins as forty and eighty drachmae. In the later Hellenistic period a bronze 'standard' existed in the Ptolemaic coinage. Silver stocks had clearly diminished in Egypt by about 210 BC and large sums are regularly quoted in papyri in bronze drachmae, without any attempt to quote their equivalent in silver. In regular payments of daily commerce silver was not used again until the mid-first century BC. It was probably at the time of the reforms of Ptolemy II and Ptolemy III that the coins came to be known by their weights in drachmae. The coin of 105 grammes, for example, might have been known as a thirty drachmae piece. The names of the denominations in drachmae would then have persisted through the various reforms that reduced the actual size of the pieces to mere tokens, and with the inflation of the late third and early second century the nominal value of the pieces as drachmae may have multiplied many times.

Bronze coins as large as those of Ptolemy II and Ptolemy III are rare, but are known at Lipara off Sicily and Olbia in south Russia in the fourth century BC. In the Hellenistic period the only parallel is in the kingdom of Syria. Antiochus IV (175-164 BC) copied the earlier Egyptian coinage in an issue of five bronze denominations at Antioch, the largest of which reaches over 70 grammes in weight. The reverse eagle underlines the connection with Egypt, and it is probable that the coins were struck at the time of his short-lived expedition to conquer Egypt in 170 BC (**271**). A little earlier, Seleucus IV (187-175 BC) struck exceptionally large bronzes at Ecbatana in Media, with an elephant reverse, and these were followed at the same mint by a similar sequence of denominations up to 40 grammes struck by the usurper Timarchus in 162 BC (**274**).

The bronze coinage of Antiochus IV is also noted for the presence of value marks, monograms of the letters AX, BX, and ΔX, indicating 1, 2 and 4 chalkoi, on clearly defined denominations at the mint of Nisibis. A further experiment in the Seleucid kingdom is the casting of the flans with scalloped or notched edges (**275**), giving the appearance of a modern metal bottle top. The purpose of this would seem to be purely decorative, and became fashionable in the mid-second century at Antioch, beginning in the reign of Seleucus IV. Casting was used to produce the flans for the Egyptian bronze denominations. They are given bevelled edges, and in later issues the sprues left on the edges show that they were cast in runs and then chopped roughly apart. An interesting technical feature, which is occasionally found elsewhere, is also to be noted. The later bronze coins often display a central conical cavity on both sides. Sometimes this can be seen to be the centre for a series of concentric striations which have survived the striking of the flan on the higher parts of the design (**297**). The most plausible explanation is that the mould for casting the flan must have been drilled in stone, or some such material, with a bit that had an open end. This would leave in the mould a small conical protrusion in the centre with the marks of the cutting edge around it. In the casting, the raised cone leaves a sunken impression in the flan with striations around. The force required to strike up the designs, particularly on flans of broad diameter, was considerable, and with the hand-held equipment it was not sufficient to completely obliterate the marks from the casting process.

Fashion in coinage

A number of factors influence the choice of designs for Greek coins, but the need for acceptability can lead to the copying of a design or elements in a design of a particularly respected coinage. The influence of the silver coinage of Alexander the Great led to the regular appearance of seated figures of many different sorts in the Hellenistic coinages, and recently there has been much discussion over the significance of the wreaths that became popular in the mid-second century BC. The wreath signifies victory, but through use as a decorative border to the design it could lose its original significance. Philip V of Macedonia introduced it onto his silver coins at the time of war with Rome at the end of the third century BC. The Athenians adopted it for their *stephanephori* (**241-4**), and in the 170s a wreath is even placed around the reverse of a tetradrachm in the name of Alexander from Erythrae in Ionia (**257**). In the middle of the century a number of cities of western Asia Minor adopted the fashion for Attic weight coinages (**258**) struck in apparent competition with the royal cistophori, which themselves also sported a wreath (**259**).

The Athenian New Style coinage introduced a remarkable set of different subsidiary marks. For over two generations three names are regularly placed in the design, two representing officials who changed annually, the third often changing several times a year. This last was presumably some more junior official directly connected with the production of a particular issue. It became common practice to place the name of the people in full in the coin design, and this mass of names from many different cities provides a great deal of information which can be linked to that from epigraphic sources to give genealogical tables of the leading families in many cities. At Athens, in addition to the names, the New Style coins carry a symbol that is often related to, and possibly was chosen by, the first name listed. In addition a letter was added to give the month of issue, in fact representing the board of prytaneis who held office for a month. Other letters apparently referred to the source of the metal from which the issue was struck. A number of coinages at this time display an array of subsidiary marks.

Another fashion of the earlier second century in western Asia Minor was the issue of tetradrachms illustrating cult images. In Macedonia, in the First Republic founded by the Romans, we find the Artemis Tauropolos from Amphipolis. At Samos, there is the statue of Hera and there are a number of issues struck in the name of the god or sanctuary, such as Athena Nikephoros at Pergamum, an issue of tetradrachms discovered in 1968 and, most recently, of Zeus Soter at Clazomenae. At Troy such issues form the currency for the confederation that centred itself upon the sanctuary of Athena Ilias.

The use of titles on coins, both by kings and by cities, is also a fashion of the second century BC that persists and grows under the Roman Empire. The various kings of Syria differentiate themselves by their adopted epithets – Antiochus IV Epiphanes Nikephoros, Antiochus V Eupator, Antiochus VI Epiphanes Dionysus, Antiochus VII Euergetes, and so forth. For cities, the expression of freedom often gained through treaty at the instigation of Rome is a matter to be celebrated on coins, and the terms 'holy' (IEPA), 'self-governing' (ΑΥΤΟΝΟΜΟΣ), and 'safe from violence' (ΑΣΥΛΟΣ) come to be widely used in Cilicia, Syria (**270**) and Phoenicia (**269**).

The coming of the Romans

The influence of Rome can of course be seen in many aspects of coinage from the fourth century onwards. Her influence in the West, culminating with the defeat of Carthage in the second Punic War (218–201 BC), brought an end to autonomous silver coinages in Italy and transformed the coinage of Carthage herself. In Greece, Rome's involvement in curtailing and ultimately breaking the power of Macedonia led to the growth in the organization of leagues in Epirus, Aetolia, Acarnania, Thessaly, Boeotia and Achaea, all of which issued federal coinage at the time when Roman influence was rising, the Thessalians coining down to the time of Julius Caesar. The affairs of Greece were settled in 196 BC after victory over Philip V, and confirmed after the final overthrow of the Macedonian monarchy in 168 BC. The suppression of resistance from the Achaean League with the destruction of Corinth in 146 BC made Roman power supreme in Greece. Thereafter, coinages in bronze abound, but in silver the only significant coinage of southern Greece was the New Style coinage at Athens. In Macedonia, the royal issues were replaced by issues from the Macedonian republics, mainly from the first with its mint at Amphipolis, and Thasos and Maronea provided a sequence of tetradrachms down to the first century BC.

In Asia Minor the treaty of Apamea confirmed freedom on a number of cities which later began to coin in silver. The kingdom of Pergamum was bequeathed to Rome in 133 BC, and the policy until the mid-first century BC of not imposing the use of denarii on the provinces led to the continuation of the cistophori as a provincial, instead of a royal, coinage, those at Ephesus using the date of 133 as the base for an era of the province. Gold coins from Ephesus (**260**), outwardly autonomous with the reverse depicting the cult image of Artemis, can be linked through these dates and subsidiary symbols to the provincial cistophori. Issues which used to be considered emergency issues at the time of the invasion of Mithradates can now be placed in the period 133-120 BC. A second group, to be dated 82-79 BC, falls in the period of entrenchment after the first war of 88-85 BC. The attempts of Mithradates to counter the expansion of Rome have left their mark on the coinages. His four-year occupation of Pergamum is illustrated by a lettered sequence A-Δ, 1-4, on gold and silver issues, and his presence in Athens is marked by his name and title appearing on the Athenian coinage (**243-4**). At Odessus in Thrace, his portrait is used for the head of Heracles on an issue of tetradrachms of Alexander type (**249**), probably in the mid 70s, and at Smyrna his portrait appears on a bronze issue during his period of rule in the area (88-85 BC).

Such disruptions to the stability of the provinces resulted in the steady decrease of silver issues from the cities, with a consequent increase of control by the Roman authorities. The Roman policy towards the end of the Republic of replacing autonomous silver coinages with provincial coinages based on autonomous issues reaches particularly strange heights in Syria. This became a Roman province in 64/3 BC with the defeat of Tigranes by Pompey, but the provincial coinage from Antioch adopted under Roman rule was in the form of posthumous tetradrachms of King Philip Philadelphus (89-84/3 BC), which continued well into the rule of Augustus down to *c*.13 BC (**278**). The patterns established in the last two centuries BC were to formulate Rome's attitude to the coinages of the eastern provinces under the empire. The changes of fashion were to give the coins themselves a very different aspect, but the emphasis on local issues of bronze coinage for local use and on provincial silver issues was to remain.

Further reading

General:

M.H. Crawford, *Coinage and money under the Roman Republic* (London, 1985)

N. Davis and C.M. Kraay, *The Hellenistic Kingdoms: Portrait Coins and History*

B.V. Head, *Historia Numorum*, Ed. 2 (London, 1911, reprinted)

G.K. Jenkins, *Ancient Greek Coins* (London, 1972)

C.M. Kraay, *Greek Coins* (London, 1966)

C.M. Kraay, *Archaic and Classical Greek Coins* (London, 1976)

M.J. Price and N.M. Waggoner, *Archaic Greek Silver Coinage: The Asyut Hoard* (London, 1976)

For more detailed study:

The immense breadth and complexity of Greek coinage has led to a very large number of publications each year. To keep up-to-date with current ideas the student needs to know how to search for particular publications. These are summarised in the periodical publication *Numismatic Literature* published by the American Numismatic Society, New York, as regular addenda to the publication of the Society's library catalogue (Boston, 1962-78). These provide an excellent guide to the available literature. Details of hoards of Greek coins are gathered in M. Thompson, O. Morkholm, C.M. Kraay (eds.), *An Inventory of Greek Coin Hoards* (New York, 1973). Additions to the list are to be found in the periodical *Coin Hoards*.

In addition, detailed bibliography of different areas is available in the German series of articles *Literaturüberblicke der griechischen Numismatik*. A full list of these is to be found in the German periodical *Chiron* 1985, p. 283.

Up-to-date surveys of recent numismatic research have been published regularly in recent years:

1960-1965 (Ed. O. Morkholm et al., Copenhagen, 1967)

1966-1971 (Ed. P. Naster et al., New York, 1973)

1972-1977 (Ed. R. Carson et al., Berne, 1979)

1978-1984 (Ed. M. Price et al., London, 1986)

Basic material:

The twenty nine volumes of the *Catalogue of Greek Coins in the British Museum* (BMC) are an excellent source of reference for material. The *Sylloge Nummorum Graecorum* series of catalogues (SNG) now exists for collections in Denmark, France, Germany, Great Britain, Greece, Sweden, and the United States. These provide an excellent illustrated guide to material.

List of illustrations

The following abbreviations have been used: AE (bronze); AR (silver); AU (gold); EL (electrum).

Plate 1

1 Ionia. EL forty-eighth, 625-600 BC
2 Ionia, EL sixth, 625-600 BC
3 Ionia, EL twenty-fourth, 625-600 BC
4 Ionia, EL third, 625-600 BC
5 Lydia, EL third, 600-550 BC
6 Lydia, EL third, countermarked, 600-550 BC
7 Lydia, EL third, 600-550 BC
8 Phocaea, EL stater, 600-550 BC
9 Miletus, EL stater, 600-550 BC
10 ? Halicarnassus, EL twelfth, c.600-580 BC
11 Phanes, ? Halicarnassus, EL stater, c.600-580 BC
12 Samos, EL half stater, 600-550 BC
13 Lydia, AU heavy stater, c.550 BC
14 Lydia, AR stater, c.550 BC
15 Lydia, AR siglos, c.520 BC
16 Darius I, AR siglos, 510-490 BC
17 Darius I, AU daric, 510-490 BC
18 Darius I, AU twelfth, 510-490 BC
19 Xerxes, AR siglos, c.480 BC

Plate 2

20 Caria, AR stater, c.530 BC
21 Caria, AR twelfth, c.525 BC
22 ? Aegean islands, AR stater, c.520BC

Plate 3

Plate 4

Plate 5

Plate 6

Plate 7

Plate 8

Plate 9

Plate 10

Index

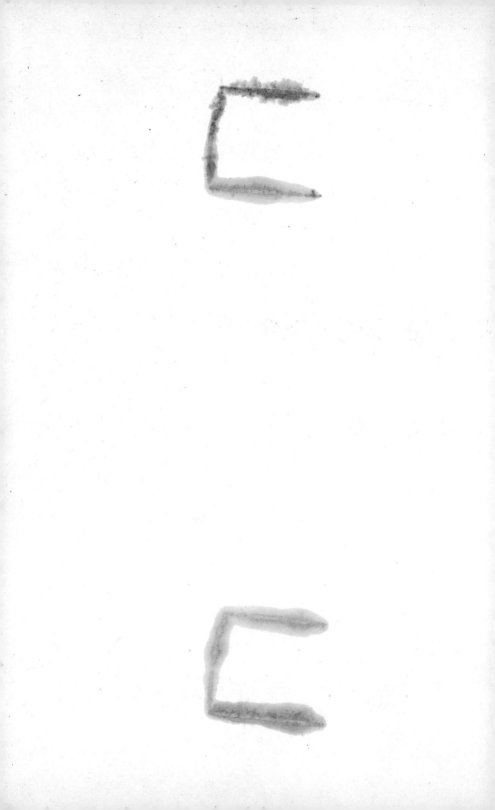